READING JOHN FOR THE FIRST TIME

Wilfrid J. Harrington, OP

Paulist Press
New York / Mahwah, NJ

Cover image by Renata Sedmakova / Shutterstock.com

Cover and book design by Sharyn Banks

Library of Congress Cataloging-in-Publication Data

Harrington, Wilfrid J.
Reading John for the first time / Wilfrid J. Harrington, OP.
pages cm
Includes bibliographical references.
ISBN 978-0-8091-4938-4 (pbk. : alk. paper) — ISBN 978-1-58768-529-3 (ebook)
1. Bible. John—Criticism, interpretation, etc. I. Title.
BS2615.52.H37 2015
226.5`06—dc23

2015022797

ISBN 978-0-8091-4938-4 (paperback)
ISBN 978-1-58768-529-3 (e-book)

Published by Paulist Press
997 Macarthur Boulevard
Mahwah, New Jersey 07430
www.paulistpress.com

Printed and bound in the
United States of America

CONTENTS

PREFACE

The first three Gospels—the Synoptics—despite distinctive characteristic features, follow a similar pattern. The Fourth Gospel—John—is notably different.

This difference is not only in the plan of the narrative. It is evident in the presentation of the person of Jesus. He is more regal throughout and speaks a language other than that of the homely Nazarene. Besides, in the Synoptics, Jesus proclaims the coming—and the presence—of the rule of God. In John, Jesus proclaims himself: Revealer of the Father and of the Father's plan of salvation.

In reading John, one must be prepared for challenge. There are, indeed, the lively narratives of the Man Born Blind (chap. 9), the Death of Lazarus (chap. 11), and the dramatic passion narrative (chaps. 18—19). On the other hand, we have the dense texts of chapters 7—8 and of the discourses (chaps. 14—16). Candidly, these are not easy to follow. One should not be discouraged. The Evangelist is, there also, pursuing his passionate endeavor to reveal the Revealer and the Revealed—Father and Son.

We should strive to listen and to hearken.

As a scripture scholar, one is always beholden to other scholars. In this instance, I acknowledge a special indebtedness to a remarkable recent commentary, *The Gospel of John*, by the scripture scholar Francis J. Moloney. A glance at the footnotes will indicate how much I appreciate his work and how much I have learned from it.

Wilfrid J. Harrington, OP

INTRODUCTION
The Fourth Gospel

According to the mainstream of early church tradition, John the Apostle, son of Zebedee and brother of James, wrote, in old age, his Gospel in Ephesus. But the tradition is not unanimous. The Fourth Evangelist, no less than the other three, despite being given a name, is anonymous. We should look to an intriguing character in the Fourth Gospel.

THE BELOVED DISCIPLE

At John 13:23, the Beloved Disciple (literally, "the one whom Jesus loved") appears for the first time. Henceforth, he will crop up regularly and always, explicitly or implicitly, in contrast to Peter. At the farewell meal, he reclined next to Jesus and passed on Peter's question to Jesus (13:23–25). He may be that "other disciple" who accompanied Peter and procured his entry into the court of the high priest (18:15–16).

He stood, prominently, at the foot of the cross—Peter being conspicuously absent (19:25–27). The Beloved Disciple reached the tomb before Peter, and though the latter was first to enter the tomb, it was the former alone who "saw and believed" (20:2–10). Chapter 21 is built around Peter and the Beloved Disciple. Although Peter has the more important role (vv. 2, 3, 7, 11), it was the other who was sensitive in faith to the presence of the risen Jesus and recognized him (v. 7). Peter asked of the Beloved Disciple, "Lord, what about him?" (v. 21). Evidently, behind the question lies the fact that the Disciple had died and a misunderstanding of a saying of Jesus is corrected (vv. 22–23). At first sight, verse 24—"This is the disciple who is testifying to these things and has written them"—would seem a formal claim to authorship. In fact, the Greek can quite well be understood in the sense that the Beloved Disciple is a witness to Jesus and source of the tradition behind the Fourth Gospel and the occasion of its writing. The Evangelist was his disciple. Who this Evangelist was, we do not know. We continue to name him conventionally "John."

In summary, the Fourth Gospel had a complex genesis and grew in stages. Yet, it shows the signs of being molded by a dominant person, who shaped the traditional material to a particular theological cast and expression. We can be sure that, for the Johannine community, someone other than he, that is, the Beloved Disciple, a disciple of the ministry (not one of the Twelve) and source of the tradition, was the greatly revered link with Jesus. He stands, in contrast to Peter, as the father figure of the Johannine group. The Fourth Gospel may have taken its final shape in Ephesus—where also the later epistles (1, 2, and 3 John) would have been written. It was probably written between 90 and 100 CE.

"THE JEWS"

It is a truism that Christianity began as a movement within Judaism. It ought to come as no surprise to find in the Fourth Gospel clear evidence of that origin. It is, indeed, a very Jewish Gospel. Naturally, Jews are frequently mentioned. The term *Jew* is used in an ethnic sense (for example, 4:9; 18:35) and in a general sense, referring to the Jewish people. What is distinctive is a broad use of "the Jews" in a pejorative sense (for example, 2:20; 5:18; 8:48; 9:18; 19:7). "The Jews" are the implacable opponents of Jesus. Indeed, Jesus himself seems no longer a Jew! What has happened is that the tension between Jesus and his Jewish opponents throughout the ministry has been projected on to the later time of conflict between Johannine disciples and the synagogue authorities. To distinguish this singular usage, it helps to place the term within quotation marks.

The Fourth Gospel is certainly not anti-Semitic—in the current sense. The Evangelist and his Christians are themselves Jews. What we have is something of a family quarrel. We may, with some confidence, discern its course. First, a claim that Jesus was Messiah made by some Jews, while not acceptable to other synagogue brothers and sisters, could be tolerated. The situation became tense when Jesus' followers began to make more daring claims on behalf of their Messiah.

The Jewish world of Jesus was pluralistic. Pharisees, Sadducees, Essenes, and Baptist disciples are but some of the groups: Jews all of them, but with marked theological differences. Initially, Christians—Jewish Christians—would have fit under the Jewish umbrella. The Jewish-Roman war of 66–70 CE changed all that. The destruction of Jerusalem and temple in 70 CE was a traumatic moment. Judaism had its back to the wall: there was no longer scope for tolerance. The pillars of Judaism were Torah (the Mosaic Law) and temple; now temple was gone. With the destruction of the temple, the priesthood had lost its *raison d'etre*. It may be assumed that, while the Pharisees were mainly responsible for the survival of Judaism, one can be reasonably sure that some of the temple priests had read the signs of the times and had made common cause with Pharisees who were building for the future. For their part, the Pharisees, in the desperate situation after the Roman victory, would have welcomed support of former priests prepared to work with them. And this would seem to be the view of the Fourth Evangelist. In John 18:3, "the chief priests and the Pharisees" are, surely, the same people as "the Jews" named up to then. "The Jews" are, in short, not contemporaries of Jesus but the leaders of a later Judaism vigorously opposed to the now distinctive Christian movement. This was during the closing decades of the first century and marks the climax of a fairly gradual development.

CONFLICT WITH "THE JEWS"

The first Johannine Christians were, all of them, Jews who lived within the synagogue structure. They acknowledged Jesus as the fulfillment of Israel's hope and strenuously proclaimed their conviction. They maintained that Jesus was immeasurably superior to all of the religious figures of Israel—even Abraham and Moses. In debate with their fellow Jews, they further pressed their claims for Jesus. He was the Word of God (1:1) who alone had seen God (1:18; 6:46). Indeed, Jesus was "making himself equal to God" (5:18; see 10:33). For non-Christian Jews, such claims were intolerable: one could not make such claims for Jesus and remain within the synagogue. The Johannine Christians found themselves expelled from the synagogue. In chapter 9 of John, the parents of the man born blind will not be drawn into the quarrel "because they were afraid of the Jews; for the Jews had already agreed that anyone who confessed Jesus to be the Messiah would be put out of the synagogue" (v. 22; see 9:34). The same evidence emerges from verses 12:42 and 16:2. One can no longer be a follower of Jesus and remain within this reestablished Judaism.

CONFLICT WITHIN

Recent study of the New Testament has brought to light not only evidence of rich pluralism but also, it has, more dramatically, unveiled evidence of tension and strife within Christian communities. There are sufficiently clear pointers to a turbulent history of the Johannine community. The Fourth Gospel and epistles witness to conflict: conflict of a Jewish-Christian group with fellow Jews and conflict within the Christian community. It is no petty squabbling. The evidence suggests that, for the most part, tension focused on the assessment of Jesus.

Significantly, the question at issue had been raised in another gospel tradition: "Who do you say that I am?" (Mark 8:29).

A bitter blow was when some within the community found the claim that Jesus was a descended heavenly being too much to take and left. "When many of his disciples heard it, they said, 'This teaching is difficult; who can accept it?'...Because of this many of his disciples turned back and no longer went about with him" (John 6:60, 66). Those who remained hardened their christological stance. For one thing, their emphasis on Jesus as one "descended" from the heavenly world came to mean that he was "not of this world" (see 17:16). Stress on the otherworldliness of Jesus meant that the significance of his life and death might be obscured—a fact that surfaces in the Johannine Epistles. These epistles tell of a further schism, again over the christological issue (see 1 John 2:18–19). And this is a very good reason why the Fourth Gospel should be taken in close association with the letters. It would seem, in fact, that the author of 1 John was largely responsible for having the Fourth Gospel accepted by the Church at large.

COMMUNITY

It emerges that the distinctive Johannine christology was hammered out in a process of making and defending claims for Jesus, a Jesus who continued to loom more and more largely not only on the community's horizon but at the heart of its life. If the Fourth Gospel grew out of the faith of a Christian community—as it surely did—it must indeed help to look to the life of the community. *Life* is used advisedly as being sufficiently broad and vague. A term such as *history* would be misleading. It is surely not possible to trace the history of a community that cannot be precisely identified in the first place. Our only sources are the Fourth Gospel and the three epistles. We must read between the lines, and what we read is a matter of discernment. What we discern may be close to the mark—or wide of it. What is encouraging is that the findings of foremost Johannine scholars approach something of a consensus. One speaks, for convenience, of a Johannine community though not thereby envisaging a single group. The movement must, of course, have started as such, but certainly by the time of the epistles (later than the Gospel) and surely, too, through the stages of the Gospel, there would have been an association of groups that may well have been geographically close.

JOHN AND THE SYNOPTICS

Some scholars have argued for a dependence of the Fourth Gospel on the Synoptics. Such a relationship is certainly not obvious. The Johannine tradition looks so sturdily independent; the Fourth Evangelist has his own style of narration and formulation. Even where it deals with matters also present in the Synoptics, there is no evident advertence to a Synoptic parallel. We may surely assume the existence of cross-currents between the Johannine and Synoptic traditions.

In regards to the number of external facts recorded, the Johannine tradition is, in many respects, poorer than the

Synoptic. But it gives a notable amount of extra information that merits respect from the historical point of view. The early stage or substratum of the Johannine tradition may be contemporaneous with the Synoptic tradition. What we have in our present John is a later stage of development with a lengthy evolution of tradition behind it. John has a special aim that is the readiest explanation of his differences with the Synoptics. Where he diverges from the Synoptic accounts, it is not only because he has a different and independent tradition at his disposal, but because he is intent above all on his own theological purpose.

LITERARY CHARACTERISTICS

The overall structure of the Fourth Gospel is notably dramatic. This skillfulness of presentation is also present in the larger individual episodes, such as the Samaritan Woman (chap. 4) and the Cure of the Blind Man (chap. 9), and the Raising of Lazarus (chap. 11). In these episodes, the reader is brought stage by stage to a full revelation of Jesus. And the reader, too, comes to an increasing certainty of faith. The longer narrative complexes illustrate the conflicts of opinion, the antagonism between belief and unbelief. At the same time, these episodes serve to present the great struggle between light and darkness, a struggle in which the powers of darkness and unbelief appear, from the outside, to be gaining the upper hand. Even in the shorter passages, such as the Wedding at Cana (2:1–11), the Cleansing of the Temple (2:13–22), and the Healing of the Official's Son (4:46–54), dramatic presentation is not lacking. Here, too, one finds the moment of suspense before the liberating vision of faith.

The Discourses

Nowhere does the difference between John and the Synoptics strike one more forcefully than in the discourses of Jesus. In the first three Gospels, the language of Jesus, in his sayings and parables, is very much the same in each Gospel. Even when there is a notable difference in parallel passages, it has to do with words, not style. With John, it is another matter. In the first place, there are no developed parables here, and the allegories of the Good Shepherd and the True Vine are unlike anything in the Synoptics. The presence of discourses has a parallel in Matthew. Style and content, however, are markedly different and underline the distinctiveness of the Johannine text.

In John, the teaching of Jesus is given mainly in a series of long and elaborate discourses: partly dialogue, partly monologue. The tendency is for initial dialogue to lead up to a monologue (for example, 3:1–21; 5:10–47). Or the dialogue may be ongoing (for example, 8:21–59). The outstanding discourses are on the Bread of Life (chap. 6) and the Farewell Discourse (chaps. 14—16). In these discourses, John does not reason in our western manner: he testifies; he affirms. He does not set out to prove a thesis by building up consecutive arguments until a conclusion is reached. Instead, his thought moves around a central point. John 14:1–24 can be taken as an example of how the thought "circles," repeating and insisting, while at the same time moving forward and upward. Again, one may instance the "parabolic discourses"—the Shepherd and the Flock (10:1–18) and the Vine and the Branches (15:1–10). Both passages are built on similar lines: first, a presentation of the matter, the "parable" (10:1–5; 15:1–2) followed by the typically Johannine development: a method of concentric thinking that flows in new circles. It is a meditative manner of thought. It is a personal style evolved through meditation on the revelation of Jesus Christ.

The Signs

A wide use of symbolism is an obvious characteristic of the Fourth Gospel. Such symbols, for example, are living water, bread of life, the vine, and the good shepherd. The method is, perhaps, best illustrated by a study of the term *sign* as used by the Evangelist. *Sign* does not necessarily denote a miraculous event. But, in practice, seven episodes, regarded as "signs," are also presented as miraculous. These are the following:

The Wedding at Cana (2:1–11)

Healing of the Official's Son at Cana (4:46–54)

Healing of a Paralytic on the Sabbath (5:1–18)

Multiplication of Loaves (6:1–15)

Jesus Walking on the Water (6:16–21)

Healing of a Man Born Blind (9:1–41)

The Raising of Lazarus (11:1–54)

And it is by contrasting *miracle* and *sign* that we come best to understand John's intention. The restoring of sight to a blind man at Siloam (9:1–12) is indeed a miracle, just like similar miracles in the other Gospels (see Matt 9:27–31). The Synoptists related such miracles for their own sake or, at most, because they manifested the messianic power of Jesus. But John is not interested in these miracles as such; his intent is in their symbolism, their significance. For him, the granting of sight to a blind man is a sign of the spiritual light that Christ, who is light (John 1:9), can give, because he viewed such actions of Jesus as visible pointers to a deeper, spiritual truth. That meaning is made explicit in chapters 6:35, "I am the bread of life," and 11:25, "I am the resurrection and the life."

Double Expressions

Another notable feature of the Fourth Gospel is the frequent use of double or ambiguous expressions. This practice involves a clever technique. Such expressions, when spoken by Jesus, are first taken by his interlocutors in the obvious or natural sense, and he proceeds to expound the deeper spiritual meaning. For example, in chapter 2:19, the "temple" of which Jesus speaks is not the building—as "the Jews" understood—but the temple of his body (2:21).

More characteristic, however, are such words as the adverb *anothen* (3:3, 7), which means "again," so understood by Nicodemus, and also "from above," the meaning really intended by Jesus. The rendering of the adverb qualifies the meaning of "birth" (3:3, 7) and this is also misunderstood by Nicodemus. In chapter 3:14, we read of the Son of Man being "lifted up." The same expression occurs in 8:28 and 12:32–33; in the latter case, a note makes clear that crucifixion is meant. The Evangelist regards the "elevation" of Jesus on the cross as a symbol of the manifestation of his "glory"—his revelation of the Father and of himself. In John's eyes, the death, resurrection, and exaltation of Jesus are aspects of one and the same mystery.

In interpreting the Fourth Gospel, we must be careful to give full weight to this technique of the Evangelist. It is important to realize that he has chosen these expressions precisely because they have more than one signification and that he really intends the two (or more) meanings of each expression. We would not be true to his mind if we were to narrow his meaning to one or other alternative. If John uses ambiguous words, it is not because he wants to be obscure or wishes to hide something. Quite the opposite is true, because what he does is to look beyond the superficial sense of an expression to a deeper meaning. This method is to be understood in much the same manner as his presentation of signs; not only the actions of Jesus, but his words, too, are "signs." It is because they are the words of Christ—"words of eternal life"—that they have a deeper meaning, and this truth can be effectively symbolized by the use of double expressions.

Irony

Jesus' opponents make statements about him that are incredulous or insulting. But these statements turn out to be meaningful in a sense the speakers had not realized. The believing reader will grasp the deeper truth. Examples: "Are you greater than our ancestor Jacob?" (4:12); "It is better for you to have one man die for the people than to have the whole nation destroyed" (11:50); "Because he has claimed to be the Son of God" (19:7) is the theological reason for "the Jews" bringing Jesus to trial. In their eyes, a false claim, but it is, ironically, true.

Explanatory Notes

Explanatory notes are frequent within the narrative. In a modern text, they might well appear as footnotes. Some examples: "'What are you looking for?' They said to him, 'Rabbi' (which translated means Teacher), 'where are you staying?'" (1:38); "'And I, when I am lifted up from the earth, will draw all people to myself.' He said this to indicate the kind of death he was to die." (12:32–33); and "Jesus said to Philip, 'Where are we to buy bread for these people to eat?' He said this to test him, for he himself knew what he was going to do" (6:5–6).

The World

The term *kosmos*, "world," appears frequently in the Fourth Gospel. Sometimes it means, simply, "created reality" (11:9; 17:5, 24; 21:25). More commonly, it refers to the world of humankind. This is the world God loves and whose salvation he desires: "For God so loved the world that he gave his only Son, so that everyone who believes in him may not perish but may have eternal life" (3:16). Jesus is Savior of this world (4:42). (See also 1:29; 6:51; 8:12; 9:5.) Distinctively

Johannine, however, is a use of *kosmos* that is emphatically negative. It is a world that did not recognize the Logos (1:10); a world that hates Jesus (7:7). It is where the power of darkness reigns (12:31; 14:30; 15:18–19). Unbelief transforms the cosmos into the ungodly world. This negative occurence of "world" is notably present in the second half of the Fourth Gospel. The Church lives in the world but is not "of the world" (17:14–16). Disciples will have to face the enmity of the world, as Jesus did. With him and through him they will overcome: "In the world you face persecution. But take courage; I have conquered the world!" (16:33).

Admittedly, this negative role of "world" is puzzling. It would seem that rejection of this unbelieving world is envisaged. Yet, there remain God's love of his world and the reassuring word: "Indeed, God did not send the Son into the world to condemn the world, but in order that the world might be saved through him" (3:17). There is the declaration of the Son regarding the moment of supreme demonstration of that love: "I, when I am lifted up from the earth, will draw all people to myself" (12:32).

The Structure

The Fourth Gospel is, essentially, the work of a thoughtful theologian and gifted storyteller—the "Evangelist." But there are indications of the hand of a redactor (editor). So, for instance, while the passage 12:36a–43 is, clearly, the conclusion of the first half of the Gospel, Jesus, unexpectedly, speaks again in 12:44–50. Again, the discourse 14:1–31 has a close parallel in 16:4b–33—arguably, two versions of the same discourse.

Then, the purpose of the Gospel, and its obvious conclusion, is given in 20:31. Chapter 21 comes as an appendix. There are other seeming discrepancies. The fact remains: the Fourth Gospel is available to us only as it stands. This is the text of our concern. This text comes to us, in the earliest manuscripts, without any indication of a structural plan. We depend, wholly, on internal scrutiny to determine a structure. One can, at best, discern a broad outline.

THE OUTLINE OF THE FOURTH GOSPEL

Prologue (1:1–18)

An introduction to the career of the incarnate Word.

The Book of Signs (1:19—12:50)

The public ministry of Jesus where, in sign and word, he shows himself to his own people as the revelation of the Father, only to be rejected.

A. The Opening Days of the Revelation of Jesus (1:19–51)
B. From Cana to Cana (2—4)
C. Jesus and the Feasts of the Jews (5—10)

The Book of Glory (13—20)

To those who accept him, Jesus shows his glory by returning to the Father in "the hour" of his crucifixion, resurrection, and ascension. Fully glorified, he communicates the Spirit of life.

A. Jesus' Final Encounter with "His Own" (13—17)
B. The Passion (18—19)
C. The Resurrection (20:1–29)

Conclusion (20:30–31)

Epilogue (21)

CHAPTER 1

THE JOHANNINE JESUS

The Fourth Gospel was a major factor in the elaboration of trinitarian theology and Christology in the councils of Ephesus (431) and Chalcedon (451). These councils were centuries later than our Gospel. Our concern is the Jesus of John. His understanding of Jesus was, of course, quite independent of these later developments. The origin of John's Christology is the Christian Easter experience of the risen Christ. The claims of the Johannine Jesus are the claims of the Christ of faith. In the Fourth Gospel, God (*ho theos*) is the Father; the Son is the one whom he has sent, his revealer. In Jesus, God has become visible; God has become historically transparent in this "Son." Jesus, in his earthly life, is revelation of the invisible Father. What John is doing is to say, simultaneously, that Jesus is fully human and is also fully the revelation of God.

HOW JOHN PRESENTED JESUS

The distinctiveness of the Johannine Jesus is evident from the first line of the Fourth Gospel. He is the incarnate Logos—the human presence of God in the world. Jesus is the new temple: the meeting-place of God and humankind—the "place" of true worship (see 2:13–22; 4:20–24); He has brought to fulfillment the feasts of Israel; he is the Light of the world (chaps. 7—9); He is the Good Shepherd who lays down his life for his sheep (chap. 10); He is the Way to the Father, the true way, the way of life (chap. 14). As genuine Vine, he is the life-source of his disciples (chap. 15). He is the one, lifted up from the earth on the cross, who draws all to himself (8:28; 12:32). He pours out the life-giving Spirit (7:37–39; 19:34–35).

As one come down from heaven, Jesus from the start seems an otherworldly figure. Admittedly, he can be found wearily by a well (4:6); He is a man who "loved Martha and her sister and Lazarus" (11:5). But these are rare flashes. It is the majestic Word-made-flesh who moves through the pages of John. The passion narrative (chaps. 18—19) effectively illustrates the distinctiveness of this Jesus. John presents the passion as the triumph of the Son of God. Jesus is firmly in control. He is the Judge who judges his judge (Pilate) and his accusers ("the Jews"). He is the King who reigns, with the cross for a throne.

The Johannine Icon

The Synoptists wrote out of their Easter faith, but they, to an extent, have allowed the historical Jesus to be seen and to speak. John, for his part, has imposed the Christ of faith upon the earthly Jesus. He has painted an icon. An icon does not aim at literal presentation; it is consciously stylized. An icon brings out the spiritual significance of the subject. The Johannine icon, then, represents the Jesus of faith, the risen Lord. As well, the Fourth Evangelist has put into the mouth of his Jesus the theological significance of what the earthly Jesus had meant. His Jesus is an icon of the Christ of faith; the words of his Jesus are words of the risen Lord. In short, the Johannine Jesus is the Christ of our postresurrection faith experience.[1]

HOW JESUS PRESENTED HIMSELF

In general, John and the Synoptics tell the same story, but tell it differently. While already in Matthew and Luke there is a tendency to stress what one might term the other-worldliness of Jesus, in John, he seems something of a sojourner from another world. In the Synoptic Gospels, Jesus' message concerns the "kingdom of God," the benevolent rule of God. In John, what Jesus preaches, what he reveals, is himself. Jesus is still concerned to make the real God known, but now, what God is can be found and seen in Jesus himself. True, it is in and through Jesus we come to know God, but the Johannine emphasis is unique: "No one has ever seen God. It is God the only Son, who is close to the Father's heart, who has made him known" (1:18).

The Sent One

For John, Jesus is the "one sent." He is the agent of the Father, empowered to speak and act in the name of the Father. As the fully accredited agent, Jesus is the bearer of God's name and power. This role of agent explains otherwise contradictory statements in the Fourth Gospel. Tension is sharpest in the contrast of two terse declarations: "The Father and I are one" (10:30); "The Father is greater than I" (14:28). When we read them in the role of agent and against other texts throughout the Gospel, we appreciate that there is no contradiction.

The Johannine Jesus is always conscious of being the "one sent."[2] His statements are unambiguous: "I seek to do not my own will but the will of him who sent me" (5:30); if he freely lays down his life, it is because "I have received this command from my Father" (10:18); he is Son, apprenticed to his Father: "The Son can do nothing on his own, but only what he sees the Father doing; for whatever the Father does, the Son does likewise" (5:19). "The Father loves the Son and shows him all that he himself is doing" (5:20). This Father has sent him into the world. It is precisely because he is agent, plenipotent representative of the Father, that he is the living presence of that Father; he has been accredited with the Father's name and power: "Believe me that I am in the Father and the Father is in me" (14:11); "Whoever has seen me has seen the Father" (14:9). He is God's Son because he is the one "whom the Father has sanctified and sent into the world"

(10:36). Jesus speaks the "I am" as the one who bears God's name and wields his power. In him, God—the everlasting one—is revealed and made present.

Revealer of the Father, Jesus is not identical with the Father. Here is where the statement, "The Father is greater than I" (14:28) makes sense. The priority of the Father comes from the fact that Jesus' power comes from him. But what is one to make of the confession, "My Lord and my God" (20:28) at the close of the Gospel? Thomas was reacting in wonder and praise to the God who was so dramatically revealed in the risen Jesus.

The Logos

A traditional starting point of Christology is the Johannine statement *ho logos sarx egeneto*—the Word became flesh, became a human person (see John 1:14). *Logos* is "word," and a word is essentially about communication; it is meant to say something. Here, God is Speaker. His Word is more than communication: it is the life-giving Word of the Creator. The Word of God is God's eternal commitment to be personally present in human history. God not only communicates; he wills to share his own life and his very self. Jesus is the concrete shape and form that God's eternal intent has taken—the self-communication of God.

As for Jesus, aware of the call of God, conscious of the fatherly love of God, he knew himself to be the one whom God has sought as his counterpart from eternity. He accepts his role as *Son*. The definitive answer to God's decision not to be alone was spoken, in freedom, by a human person. To Jesus, God could say, "My Son" and hear the spontaneous response, "*Abba*." The mystery of Jesus is that, in him, God communicates himself in a full and unrestricted manner. And the divinity of Jesus means that he is the human person in whom God is wholly present. He is the manifestation and presence of God himself in the world.

Throughout the Gospel, Jesus displays omniscience, refers to his presence with the Father, and behaves like the risen Lord. The declaration, "The Father and I are one" (10:30) is not intended as a metaphysical statement on the unity of Father and Son. Rather, John's concern is a unity of revelation between Father and Son. As the one sent and as Revealer, Jesus is the eternal Word of God, the eternal Son of God. Jesus of Nazareth is the Logos of God in person and he is Logos in his humanness.

As the one who makes God uniquely present, as Revealer of God, Jesus is God's only Son. Perhaps the prologue of Hebrews puts the matter more understandably. In the past, God spoke at various times and in many ways through the prophets. In the fullness of time, he has spoken in the person of his Son—who is "the reflection of God's glory and the exact imprint of God's very being" (Heb 1:3). Jesus is the manifestation and presence of God in our world. The mystery abides—and we should respect it. Jesus of Nazareth is Son of God. "He became human without reservation, a human being among human beings. At the same time he is God's Son, again without reservation or distinction."[3] This is the astonishing implication of the following statement: "The Word became flesh and lived among us" (John 1:14).

I AM

Distinctively, in the Fourth Gospel, there is a series of "I am" sayings.[4] The majority of these "I am" sayings are with a predicate (for example, "I am the bread of life"). In all such cases, Jesus is not describing who he is, but what he does. In the example above, he declares that he nourishes with a bread that gives and sustains (eternal) life. Then there are the four absolute "I am" sayings (8:24, 28, 58; 13:19). In fact, John 8:28 makes the point: "When you have lifted up the Son of Man, then you will realize that I am he." Each time, there is an echo of the divine name of Exodus 3:14, or more immediately, of Isaiah 43:10–11. Jesus is declaring: "I am the bearer of God's name and power."

Glory

In the Old Testament, the manifestation of God to the people is expressed in the term *kabod* (Exod 33:22)—rendered in the Septuagint as *doxa* ("glory"). The "glory of God" is, then, the manifestation of the reality of God. The incarnate Son is the Revealer of God. His "glory" is the reflection of the "glory" of the Father (John 1:14). Where Jesus ultimately reveals the "glory of God" and his own "glory" is on the cross—this is "the hour." By his death on the cross, his unconditional gift of himself in love, Jesus manifested that the "glory" of God, the true nature of God, is love. As the Sent One, he, on the cross, was himself "glorified"—fully manifested. His consummate deed of love showed forth the Father as who he is and showed himself to be the faithful Son. He made startlingly clear the unambiguous concern of our God: "God's love was revealed among us in this way: God sent his only Son into the world so that we might live through him" (1 John 4:9).

The Hour

At the Cana wedding, Jesus declared abruptly, "My hour has not yet come" (John 2:4). This "not yet" builds a tension into the narrative: a sequence of events leading to an "hour." A climax is reached in 12:23—"The hour has come for the Son of Man to be glorified." This is the hour of crucifixion. Distinctively Johannine is the designation of Jesus' death as exaltation—"lifting up" (3:13–14). The same expression in 8:28 and 12:32 points to the crucifixion of Jesus. This "lifting up" is the self-gift of Jesus for the life of the world (3:14–15). By characterizing crucifixion as exaltation and glorification, John clearly thinks of cross and resurrection as one.

In John 13:1—"Jesus knew that his hour had come to depart from this world and go to the Father. Having loved his own who were in the world, he loved them to the end"—Jesus declares that his fulfillment of "the hour" will be the supreme manifestation of his love for "his own." *Eis telos*, "to the end," means not only to the end of his life but, also, "utterly," without limit. In this loving gift of self, he, the Revealer, makes God known—the true God (3:16–17).

RESPONSE

Faith

The challenge of the Revealer is stark but comforting. The God revealed by the One sent to reveal him is a God of infinite love: "He who did not withhold his own Son" (Rom 8:32). But this is the message not only of John, not only of the New Testament, but of the Bible. There is no other God than this God: Father of our Lord Jesus Christ.

Faith has a supremely important place in John's theology. Faith, of course, is equally emphasized by Paul, but the accent is different. For one thing, John prefers the verb *to believe* while Paul favors the noun *faith.* Perhaps John wants to stress that faith is less an internal disposition than an active commitment; but surely Paul would concur. More significant is the fact that, for Paul, faith in the crucified and risen Lord is all-important. John projects this faith on to his account of the earthly work of Jesus and shows it unfolding in personal encounter with the Redeemer during his earthly life. He is careful, though, to bring out its bearing on the time after Easter as he does in Jesus' concluding statement: "Blessed are those who have not seen and yet...believe" (John 20:29). Still, by his projecting Christian faith into the time of Jesus' ministry, John can strikingly and effectively describe exactly the beginning and the growth of faith, the motives that inspire it, and the dangers that threaten it. He can show that Jesus himself demands faith as the one thing necessary for salvation and can make it clear that faith is faith in Jesus as the one in whom God has revealed himself. And he also brings out that faith is rooted in this historical and incarnational revelation. It is precisely because of this incarnational dimension that Paul and John are at one in asserting that faith must become effective in love. "For in Christ Jesus neither circumcision nor uncircumcision counts for anything; the only thing that counts is faith working through love" (Gal 5:6). And, in John, brotherly/sisterly charity becomes the "new commandment" of Jesus (John 13:34–35).

The most distinctive and the most frequent Johannine faith expression is *pisteuin eis*, "to believe in." The usage brings out the most marked characteristic of Johannine faith—faith is directly, exclusively to the person of Jesus. To believe means to receive and accept Jesus' self-revelation. It means to attach oneself to him, in personal union, in order to receive from him eternal life; it means total commitment to him. It is so much more than trust or confidence in him. The believer can have the fullest assurance as one finds, in the very object of one's faith, the deepest motive for and the surest foundation of one's faith. For this Son is attested by the Father, and is continually attested in the apostolic testimony.

The personal union of the believer with Christ is also expressed by other terms that can stand for Johannine faith. It emerges clearly in the parallelism of John 6:35 that "to believe" in Jesus is to come to him: "I am the bread of life. Whoever comes to me will never be hungry, and whoever believes in me will never be thirsty." Faith can also be described as "hearing" the voice or the words of Jesus—hearing and obeying. The believer abides in the Word—and in Jesus himself (8:31). Believing is also seeing. More than any other New Testament writer, John laid stress on faith as vision; it is a true vision of God, of Truth. Faith and knowledge are often associated, but they are not identical. "Faith," whose object is a person, can certainly grow into "knowledge," for, in biblical thought, "to know" is always an act that institutes or reinforces fellowship. Knowledge comes through faith, and faith should grow into knowledge—a more intimate relationship with Father and Son. And because the revelation of God in Christ is preeminently the revelation of his love, there is the closest possible connection between faith and love.

Notes

1. Anthony J. Hanson, *The Prophetic Gospel* (Edinburgh: T & T Clark, 1991).

2. A list of occurrences illustrates how pervasive is this emphasis: 3:17, 34; 4:31; 5:19–23, 24, 30, 37; 6:29, 38, 39, 44, 57; 7:16, 18, 29, 33; 8:16, 18, 26, 29, 42; 10:36; 12:44, 45, 49; 13:20; 14:24; 15:21; 16:5; 17:3, 8, 18, 21, 23, 25; 20:21.

3. Udo Schnelle, *Theology of the New Testament* (Grand Rapids, MI: Baker Academic, 2009), 674.

4. See John 6:20, 35, 48, 51; 8:12, 24, 28, 58; 9:35–37; 10:7, 9, 11, 14, 25; 13:19; 14:6, 11; 15:1, 5; 18:37.

CHAPTER 2

THE BEGINNING

THE PROLOGUE (1:1–18)

The Prologue of the Fourth Gospel, a hymn, tells us that Jesus Christ is the incarnation of the Word and introduces the basic themes (life, light, darkness, truth, witness, glory, the world) that will be developed throughout the Gospel. It functions as an overture. Since it only affirms, it cannot be fully understood until the Gospel as a whole has been read.

The first part of the passage (vv. 1–11) presents the Son as the Word who brings life from God and as the light who reveals God. The Word was eternally present with God, the creative Wisdom of God (vv. 3–5, 9). The Baptist is a voice that sounds, summoning "all" to faith in that Word present in Jesus (vv. 6–8). The unbelieving world and the Jewish people turned from the light (vv. 9–11)—a negative response that will recur throughout the Gospel.

The second part (vv. 12–18) notes the positive response leading to a sharing in life, a sharing that will make believers children of God. This has come about because the heavenly Word took on our human existence and "pitched his tent" among us. Those who have received him will have seen his "glory": his filial love for his Father and the divine life that he possesses as Son, and the revelation of that love and life. Those who believe in him receive lavishly of his fullness. They have the gift of truth ("grace and truth"): the revelation of divine life and love as it is a living reality in the Son. And all because the Son alone can make the Father known—for he alone is "the reflection of God's glory and the exact imprint of God's very being" (Heb 1:3).

The Prologue depicts Jesus primarily as the one who manifests the Father to men and women. Since he alone was with God (v. 1) and since he alone has seen God (v. 18), he alone could reveal the full truth about God. Unlike the Synoptists who presented Jesus as the Messiah who inaugurates the kingdom of God, John will continue in the rest of the Gospel to present Jesus primarily as the Revealer of the Father and of the Father's plan of salvation.

"In the beginning was the Word": the opening words of John's Gospel recall Genesis 1:1. In the Old Testament, God's Word manifested him in creation, in deeds of power, in prophecy. Perhaps even more evocatively, behind John's *logos* ("word") and the Prologue as a whole, is the striking personification of Wisdom, notably in Job 28; Proverbs 8; Sirach 24; Baruch 3:9—4:4; Wisdom 7:22—8:1. The intimate relationship of Wisdom with God is expressed in a remarkable manner in Wisdom 7:25–26:

> For she is a breath of the power of God,
> and a pure emanation of the glory of the
> Almighty...
> For she is a reflection of eternal light,
> a spotless mirror of the working of God,
> and an image of his goodness.

Much of this is echoed in the Prologue. What is most significant is that Wisdom is best understood as a communication of God—and *logos* ("word") is essentially about communication.

John shows that Jesus Christ, the incarnate Word, is the ultimate revelation of God. The term, *logos*, is a signal that a word of revelation will be spoken. The Word was "with God" (John 1:1)—was in relationship with God; yet, Word and God are distinct. The Word makes God known in creation and in the human story. The Word gives true life; a life that is authentic light, illuminating and giving direction to the human way. The Word came into the world, came among his own people only to be ignored and rejected (vv. 10–11). Some, however, received the Word, by believing in Jesus. These were made children of God—here and now. These can see the revelation of God in his Son, Jesus Christ.

"And the Word became flesh and lived among us" (v. 14): the Word entered our history. "He lived among us" is, literally, "he pitched his tent among us"; John recalls Yahweh's dwelling among the Israelites in the Tent of Meeting (Exod 33:7–11). "Glory" (*kabod*) is another expression of God's presence (see Exod 40:34; 1 Kgs 8:11)—the manifestation of Yahweh to his people. "We have seen his glory" (John 1:14); John uses *doxa*, the Greek rendering of the Hebrew word. To gaze on the incarnate Word was to see the revelation of the Divine in the human story.

The "glory" of the Word is the full revelation of the Divine. While the Torah of Moses was revelation and gift (*charis*), it has been replaced by a greater gift—a gift in place of a gift (v. 17). The fullness of gift, the definitive revelation of God, has taken place in Jesus Christ. Though Israel might claim that great ones like Abraham and Moses had seen God, it is the only Son who has truly known him (v. 18). "There is only one historical figure who has told the story of God's way with the world: the only begotten Son. Throughout the story that is about to be told the Son's attention will be unbrokenly focused on the Father."[1]

THE FIRST DAYS OF JESUS' MINISTRY (1:19–51)

The Book of Signs (1:19—12:50) opens with the beginning of Jesus' ministry. The passage falls into a pattern of four days: 1:19–28, 29–34, 35–42, 43–51. The phrase "the next day" in verse 29 indicates that the questioning of the Baptist happened on day one. The first part of the passage (vv. 19–28) is the Baptist's vehement negative testimony: he is not the Messiah! Nor is he Elijah—traditionally, on the basis of Malachi 3:1; 4:5, expected to precede the Messiah. And he is not the prophet-like-Moses, another messianic precursor (see Deut 18:15, 18). He is a voice, only a heraldic voice—and yet the solemn voice of the wilderness prophet of Isaiah 40:3–5. If he baptizes, it is with water: an acknowledgment that one has repented. He is no more than a slave whose task it is to untie his master's sandal; and he feels unworthy even of that. There is polemic here. Not John himself, but disciples of the Baptist who still claimed John as Messiah are being put in their place (see Acts 19:1–4).

On day two (vv. 29–34), the Baptist bore witness to Jesus as the Lamb of God and Son of God. He is "the Lamb of God who takes away the sin of the world" (v. 29). The operative phrase is "of God"; in biblical thought, only God takes away or forgives sin (see Mark 2:7). By "Lamb of God," the Baptist has in mind the Passover lamb (John 19:14). He may, too, have in mind the Servant of the Lord who is compared to a lamb in Isaiah 53:7–12. For that matter, within the broader sacrificial system, a lamb figured regularly in rites of reconciliation and communion after sin. More than likely, the Evangelist had all of this rich background in mind. In any event, Jesus is the one who will destroy the sin that envelops humankind, but he does so as Lamb of God. He is the Son of God on whom the Spirit descended and rested—he has permanent possession of the Spirit (see Isa 11:2; 42:1). He will "baptize" by sharing his Spirit. The Evangelist knows that the glorified Jesus bestowed the Spirit (John 20:22).

On the third day (vv. 35–42), two disciples of the Baptist "followed" Jesus; in the Gospels, *akolouthein*, "to follow," means discipleship. Andrew and Simon were now Jesus' disciples. This has implications for the view that Jesus himself had been a disciple of the Baptist. Two titles emerge: "Rabbi" (v. 37) and "Messiah" (v. 41). These are inadequate titles. Even "Messiah" does not measure up to the status of the Jesus of the Prologue, nor to the Baptist's Lamb of God and Son of God. "What are you looking for?" Jesus asks, and bids the seekers "come and see" (vv. 38–39). To "come to" Jesus (see 3:18–21) and to "see" him (see 14:9) is the active movement toward the person of the Lord, and the understanding in faith of who he is. Though the first to answer the call was Andrew, attention focuses on the initiative of Jesus who designated (by a significant change of name) Peter for a future supportive role in the Christian community.

On the fourth day (vv. 43–51), "Jesus decided to go to Galilee"; the initiative passes from the Baptist to him. He called a disciple—Philip. For Philip, Jesus is "him about whom Moses in the law and also the prophets wrote" (v. 45)—a manifestly traditional understanding of messiahship. Nor is Nathanael's "Rabbi, you are the Son of God! You are the King of Israel!" (v. 49) any more than an expression of Jewish messianic hope. All the titles in verses 38–49 fall short of the true Johannine assessment.[2] In Genesis 28:12–17, Jacob dreamt of a stairway linking heaven and earth; ascending and descending "angels" symbolized the contact between God and his earthly creation. The place of the vision was Bethel ("house of God")—the "gate of heaven." Here in verse 51 the Son of Man—Jesus' self-designation—is now the gate of heaven, the communication between God and humankind. This is who he truly is.

FROM CANA TO CANA (2:1—4:54)

The title of this section is apposite because the second Cana miracle (4:43–54) is firmly linked with the story of Jesus' first visit to Cana: "Now this was the second sign that Jesus did after coming from Judea to Galilee" (4:54).

First Miracle of Cana (2:1–12)

The first character in the story, the mother of Jesus, initiated the action with her implied request: "They have no wine." Jesus' response was abrupt: "Woman, what concern is that to you and to me?" It draws a sharp line between Jesus and his mother. The second part of the response underlines this and suggests the reason: "My hour has not yet come" (vv. 3–4). The "hour" of Jesus, which unfolds throughout the Gospel, is at the pleasure of the Father. The mother stands outside the world of Father and Son. All the more surprising, then, is the mother's reaction: "His mother said to the servants, 'Do whatever he tells you'" (v. 5). Wholly unaware of her son's role in God's design, she nevertheless demands that anything he asks should be done. "She is the first person in the narrative to show, at the level of the action of the story, that the correct response to the person of Jesus is trust in his word...She trusts unconditionally, indeed even in face of apparent rejection and rebuke, in the efficacy of the word of Jesus."[3]

The water "for the Jewish rites of purification" turned into wine, symbolizes the old order that yields its place to the new. For the Evangelist, the narrative is the symbol of something that occurs throughout the whole of Jesus' ministry—the manifestation of the "glory" of Jesus. Revelation in John is the self-revelation of Jesus (ultimately, revelation of the Father); all the rest stems from this. The significance of the wine is that it is Jesus' gift, a sign that comes from him and points to him. As a gift of Jesus, the wine is given at the end; so precious and copious, it is the eschatological gift of the Messiah. The Evangelist is not referring to any particular gift (such as the Eucharist) but to Jesus himself as Revealer. If at this, "the first of his signs," Jesus "revealed his glory; and his disciples believed in him" (v. 11) this was but a beginning. The full manifestation will not be until "the hour." The disciples have much, very much, to learn.

Cleansing the Temple (2:13–21)

The cleansing of the temple that John has set at an early stage of Jesus' ministry is, more credibly, put by the Synoptists at the close of the ministry (Matt 21:12; Mark 11:15–18; and Luke 19:45). What matters is not when it happened but what it means. Jesus passed judgment on the Jewish sacrificial system. By word and deed, in the fashion of Old Testament prophets (Jer 7:11; Mal 3:1), he protests against the profanation of God's house and signals that its messianic purification is at hand. "The Jews"—the hostile religious authorities—recognize that Jesus' action was the deed of one who was a prophet and claimed to be Messiah.

John spelled out the significance of the deed. He recalled the words of the psalmist: "Zeal for your house that has consumed me" (Ps 69:9). The symbolic action had been predicted for the messianic age by Zechariah: "There shall no longer be traders in the house of the LORD of hosts on that day" (14:21). After the resurrection, the full meaning of what Jesus did and said became clear to his followers (John 2:17, 22). Jesus, the risen Messiah, had taken the place of the temple and all it stood for. The center of God's presence among his people is no longer a place; it is henceforth a person (see 4:21–24). The new sanctuary is the risen body of Jesus. In this new temple dwells the fullness of the Spirit. And that Spirit comes to those who believe, and dwells with them so that they, in their turn, become temples of God.

Jesus and Nicodemus (3:1–21)

The dialogue with Nicodemus treated of new birth. Nicodemus, "a Pharisee" and "a ruler of the Jews" came to Jesus "by night." He came out of darkness toward the light. He was well disposed but was blinkered by his theology (v. 9). This is the first step in Nicodemus's journey to faith (see 7:50–52; 19:39–42). Jesus played on the double meaning of *anothen*: "again" or "from above"; typically, John intends both meanings. True to the procedure of the Gospel, Nicodemus understood the statement of Jesus at its surface level (v. 4); Jesus then explained that he meant spiritual rebirth from above. His baptism, which brings about this rebirth, is not in water only—as was the baptism of John—but of "water and Spirit" (v. 5). The Christian reader would appreciate the need of both ritual water baptism and the spiritual experience of the "Spirit." Then comes an enigmatic reference to the death of Jesus (vv. 14–15) and a clear statement of the marvelous love of God (vv. 16–18).

In verse 14, John gives a double significance to the verb *to be lifted up*. First, it means the physical fact of being raised up on the cross, just as the bronze figure of a serpent was raised by Moses over the stricken Israelites (see Num 21:4–9). Paradoxically, Jesus' death will also be his elevation and his "glorification": the supreme moment of revelation. Like the bronze serpent of old, the Son of Man will be the effective sign of salvation for all who look on him with trust.

Verses 16–21 of John develop what had gone before. The hope of salvation offered through the descent and exaltation of the Son of Man is now traced back to its ultimate source: God's marvelous love. It was God who set the process in motion, wishing that the world might be rescued from sin. Verse 16 ("God so loved the world . . . ") is the very foundation of the Gospel. Together with 1:14 ("the Word became flesh") and 12:32 ("I, when I am lifted up from the earth, will draw all people to myself"), it constitutes the "good news" proclaimed by John.

God's love reaches out to all of humankind—that is its range. The expression of his love in the uniquely precious gift of his Son is the measure of its depth. The Father has given his only Son to the world out of love. It is the Father, therefore, who initiates the work of human redemption. John underlines the fact that Jesus is the object of all the love of the Father when he refers to Jesus as the "only" Son. Verse 17 develops this idea. God's love is shown by sending his Son on a mission of salvation. He had not been sent to judge, that is, to condemn; he had come to save. A condition must be fulfilled on the human side—we must believe in Jesus as the only Son of God, the Revealer of the Father. We must accept Jesus totally for who and what he is. Faith is a movement toward Jesus, a movement that leaves one open to the "life" that comes uniquely from him.

Yet, not everyone will benefit from the loving initiative of God. Some, by hardening their hearts against belief in Jesus, will seal their own condemnation (vv. 18–21). Jesus brings judgment with him, necessarily; he is like a light that shines into the heart of each person, and the way we react to this light determines our destiny. If in loving darkness, deceit, and selfish ways we turn willfully from God's light, we cannot come to God; we renounce the right to be called his children. For John, salvation or damnation begins already here on earth, according to one's acceptance or rejection of Jesus, the only Son of God. The essential judgment is not passed by Jesus (or by the Father), but is implied in the choice we make when we are confronted by him. Is it really as cut and dried as this? Here the dualistic tendency of the Fourth Gospel is evident.

Like Deuteronomy with its doctrine of the Two Ways (Deut 30:15–20)—"See, I have set before you today life and prosperity....If you obey the commandments of the LORD your God...then you shall live....But if your heart turns away...you shall perish....I call heaven and earth to witness against you today that I have set before you life and death"—the Fourth Gospel is very clear. The choice is stark. In John, we must come to the Light or turn away; there is no gray area.

In each case, Deuteronomy and John, the statement is rhetorically powerful. Happily, the Synoptists and Paul (and the biblical writers in general) are more alert to the fact that life is much more complex. More often than not our response in discipleship embraces failure. One finds support in the vulnerable Jesus of Mark. Notoriously, the Jesus of Luke is a friend of sinners (see Luke 15). There is our comfort. With their help, one can live with John's Jesus.

Jesus and the Baptist (1:22–36)

Verses 22–36 provide information about Jesus not found elsewhere in the gospel tradition. He moved into the Judean countryside and engaged in a ministry of baptism while, at the same time, John the Baptist was active in Samaria. Jesus was proving more successful than the Baptist. This may in some measure parallel Matthew 11:2–6. At any rate, it would suggest that Jesus had operated as a disciple of the Baptist.[4]

In chapter 3:27–30, the Baptist bears his final witness to Jesus. Earlier (1:19–23), John had forcefully asserted that he was not the Messiah. Yet, he is one sent—to prepare the way of the Messiah. His role is analogous to that of the best man at a wedding. While acknowledging his subordinate role, he rejoices in the presence of the bridegroom. "I must decrease": John graciously departs the stage. He is one who demonstrates openness to the Word of Jesus. In verses 31–36, the narrator adds his comment. God speaks his word of revelation through the testimony of the bridegroom, the Sent One. Whoever receives the testimony of Jesus acknowledges that God is reliable, trustworthy. The words Jesus speaks are God's words and God is the source of the measureless gift of the Spirit. In verse 35, the Father's love for the Son is, for the first time, stated explicitly. It was implicit in the "only Son" of verse 16.

While revelation had been the theme of verses 31–35, the passage concludes with the theme of life and judgment (v. 36). The believer in the Son has eternal life—a favorite Johannine theme. The Father sent Jesus, and therefore, Jesus is the bearer of the divine name and authority. For us, everything depends on the stance we adopt toward him. The one who will not believe must endure "God's wrath"—a traditional phrase. What is inferred is not a divine emotion, such as anger, but God's objective judgment that we are estranged from him through our own fault. One finds greater comfort in Paul: "God proves his love for us in that while we still were sinners Christ died for us" (Rom 5:8).

Throughout chapters 2:1—3:36, there is a response to Jesus from within Israel, the representatives of Israel being "the Jews," Nicodemus, and the Baptist. "Within the narrative, therefore, 'the word of Jesus' has been the place where the characters in the story encounter what God is doing in and through Jesus. By this criterion 'the Jews' demonstrate a total lack of faith while the faith of Nicodemus is limited by his determination to understand Jesus according to his own categories. Finally, John the Baptist sees himself as friend of the bridegroom, rejoicing to hear his voice. He shows an openness to the word of Jesus, cost what it may: 'He must increase but I must decrease'" (v. 30).[5]

The Samaritan Woman (4:1–54)

In chapters 2—3, there were responses to Jesus from within Israel. The encounter with the Samaritan woman is a response from outside Israel. Notably, 4:4 states that "he *had* to go through Samaria." Jesus' move beyond Israel followed a divine design. The Fourth Gospel is a gospel of personal relationships. Jesus speaks of his own relationship with his Father, with disciples, and of the relationship of disciples among themselves (for example, 15:1–17). He also reveals himself in relationship with individuals, for example, with Nicodemus (chap. 3), with a blind man (chap. 9), and here, with a Samaritan woman. He takes the initiative in revealing himself while they discover who he is and what he means to them. Our passage is an invitation to faith.

Noteworthy is the contrast between Nicodemus and the Samaritan woman. Nicodemus is Jewish in race and religion, a Pharisee, male in an androcentric society. The woman is ethnically half-caste, heretical, socially and culturally inferior, and ritually unclean. Yet, in contrast to Nicodemus, a teacher who came by night and faded away, leaving Jesus talking to himself, she engaged in lively debate with him in the full light of day and came to faith in Jesus.[6]

A weary Jesus sat by a well in hostile Samaria—a rare glimpse of his vulnerable humanness. "How is it that you, a Jew, ask a drink of me, a woman of Samaria?" (4:9)—a world of meaning crammed into a single question. Why this breach of convention that a man should so casually address a lone woman? The disciples, later, could not hide their scandal at such conduct: "They were astonished that he was speaking with a woman" (v. 27). Furthermore, a Jew ought to know better than to ask a favor of a Samaritan woman! But the woman had spoken in response to Jesus' request for a drink, and a dialogue was afoot. In a striking switch, Jesus moved from asking the woman for a drink of water to offering her a drink (v. 10).

The woman, intrigued by Jesus' offer of "living water," forgot her antagonism and spoke to him again. He had offered fresh water—where is that flowing spring? The "Jew" of verse 9 has become "Sir" (v. 11); she suggests (sarcastically, no doubt) that he may be greater than "our father Jacob." The "living water" theme exemplifies the Johannine technique of double-expression: a word of Jesus is taken by his interlocutor at its first, superficial level; Jesus then goes on to draw out its deeper meaning—as in the encounter with Nicodemus. Here, he explained that he was not offering spring water but life-giving water that is a gift of God. It is the word of revelation that becomes a life-giving spring within the believer. The woman—though she did not really understand—was open to Jesus' offer: a necessary aspect of faith.

When Jesus disclosed his awareness of her irregular marital life (a factual statement, not a laying bare of her sinfulness), the woman saluted him as a "prophet" (vv. 16–19). She has already come a long way. He then spoke to her of the new age when true worship will no longer be that of Gerizim (the Samaritan holy mountain) or of Jerusalem. Jesus himself will be the temple, the focus of worship "in spirit and truth"—Jesus reveals a God and Father who is to be worshipped with total commitment. God seeks such worshippers. The woman expressed her hope in a Messiah who would show her all that Jesus had been telling her. Jesus acknowledged himself to be that Messiah (v. 26). "I am" (*ego eimi*) recalls Exodus 3:14 and echoes Isaiah 43:10; 45:18, where it refers to the living presence of God among his people. For John, Jesus as the "one sent" is that presence. The woman went in haste to tell her people that she had met with the Messiah (see v. 29). But she had understood only at the level of her traditional expectation. Still, there had been progress. At first, Jesus was "a Jew," then, more respectfully, "Sir." The suspicion that he might be "greater than our father Jacob" introduced a new note. Rapidly, he was "prophet" and, finally, "Messiah." The narrative has been of a coming to faith, albeit imperfect faith. Perhaps Christians can identify with the woman. We need to grow in our understanding of Jesus. To let him into our lives can be embarrassing. His light shows up what is within us, lighting areas we would prefer to leave in the dark. Above all, we learn that we know him by personal encounter and that we can have from him the water of life.

The disciples, who had gone to buy food, were *scandalized* to find Jesus talking with a woman—alone (*solus cum sola!*). We note already that sad—disastrous—Christian obsession with sex, the consistent devaluation of women. "Food" is a typically Johannine double expression and the disciples misunderstood. The "food" of Jesus is to do the Father's will, to complete his work. He does so as "one sent" (see 1:14, 18, 34; 2:16; 3:16–17, 35–36). And, seeing the Samaritans (alerted by the woman's story) thronging to him, he described his mission as "harvest": the Samaritans are ripe for harvesting. The disciples were sent to continue the missionary labor already initiated by the Baptist and Jesus (v. 38).

Many of the Samaritans had believed in the testimony of the woman. They came to a deeper faith as they heard his word, as they encountered Jesus. Now they "know" him to be the universal Savior. They have reached authentic faith: they have believed because of the word of Jesus. Their declaration to the woman: "It is no longer because of what you said that we believe" (v. 42) does not imply imperfect faith on her part. Instead "this woman is the first and only person (presented) in the life of Jesus through whose words of witness a group of people is brought to 'come and see' and 'to believe in Jesus.'"[7] The whole passage becomes a sophisticated catechesis on the origin and growth of Christian faith.

The Second Cana Miracle (4:46–54)

The healing of an official's son is a variant of a Synoptic story of the healing of the centurion's servant (Matt 8:5–13; Luke 7:1–10). Jesus crossed from Samaria to Galilee and came to Cana; the reader is reminded of the "sign" that Jesus had formerly worked there. The "royal official" (4:46) was, most likely, a Gentile. "Unless you see signs and wonders you will not believe" (v. 48)—again the question of partial or authentic faith is introduced. As at verse 2:5, a rebuke was ignored (v. 49). The man "believed the word" of Jesus—the assurance that his son would live (v. 50). He had believed; he came to "know" that the word was efficacious. Compare verse 4:42—the Samaritans "believed" and "knew." The man's household believed along with him. A community of believers had come into being (v. 53).

CONCLUSION

Chapters 2—4 of John have to do with coming to faith in Jesus. The criterion is laid out in chapter 2:1–11: the mother of Jesus believed in the word of her Son (2:5); Jesus manifested his "glory" and the disciples believed (2:11). This is the yardstick that measures responses to Jesus from within Judaism (2:13—3:36) and from without (chap. 4). Also, in these chapters, the Prologue's promise of the life-giving power that comes from "believing" and "receiving" the Word-made-flesh is played out in the story of Jesus as people come to accept his word.

The Prologue introduced a Word eternally present with God and now spoken into our world. That Word became flesh in Jesus. He is, henceforth, the revelation of God—that revelation, his "glory." There is a greater gift than Torah, God's word of old. The Son knows the Father and has made him known. The Baptist pointed to Jesus as Lamb of God and Son of God. Others acknowledged him to be Messiah and King of Israel. These are titles within the perspective of Jewish messianic hope. Jesus presented himself as Son of Man, the way of communication between God and the world.

Enter the first believer in the Johannine understanding of faith. "Do whatever he tells you": the mother of Jesus had placed total trust in his word. Jesus' first "sign" was a manifestation of himself as Revealer—the symbol, his copious gift of wine. The water at the wedding had been "for the Jewish rites of purification"; the old order had been transformed. This is underwritten in the cleansing of the temple. The temple, too, will cease to be. The risen Lord will henceforth be the dwelling place of God. In dialogue with "a leader of the Jews," Jesus spoke of new birth from above, birth to eternal life. This will be when the Son of Man had been "lifted up" in death. His death is the supreme moment of the revelation of God's love: the sending of his Son for the salvation of the world. The Baptist reappeared to voice his final testimony. Then he bowed, gracefully, from the stage.

Following a series of responses from within Israel, came responses from without: from a Samaritan woman and Samaritan villagers. The lively story of encounter with the woman is a catechesis on the growth of faith. From the first hostile "Jew," the woman progressed to "Sir," "greater than Jacob," "prophet," and "Messiah." The Samaritan villagers first came to believe in Jesus "because of the woman's testimony." They attained full faith in "the Savior of the world" on the basis of his word. With the second Cana miracle and the faith of a household, a community of believers had come into being. As the Prologue had promised, those who believed in and received the Word-made-flesh became children of God.

Notes

1. Francis J. Moloney, *The Gospel of John*, Sacra Pagina 4 (Collegeville, MN: Liturgical Press, 1998), 41.

2. This is the first instance of a recurring pattern. Again and again Jesus is inadequately estimated until, at the climax, he is

recognized and acknowledged for who he really is. This is a distinctive Johannine feature, discerned by Francis Moloney and brilliantly presented throughout his commentary.

3. Moloney, *The Gospel of John*, 68.

4. See Wilfrid J. Harrington, *Jesus Our Brother: The Humanity of the Lord* (Mahwah, NJ: Paulist Press, 2010), 13–15.

5. Moloney, *The Gospel of John*, 107.

6. Michael Mullins, *The Gospel of John: A Commentary* (Dublin: Columba Press, 2003), 131–32.

7. Sandra M. Schneiders, *Written That You May Believe: Encountering Jesus in the Fourth Gospel* (New York: Crossroad, 1999), 142.

CHAPTER 3

JESUS AND THE FEASTS

The climax of the Jewish War of 68–70 CE, the destruction of Jerusalem and the temple and the near obliteration of Judaism, was traumatic, not only for Jews but for Christians and, in particular, Jewish Christians. As a Jewish Christian, writing out of and for a Jewish-Christian community, Matthew, like all Jews, had to face up to a radical challenge to Jewish identity. There were stark questions: Where is Israel now? Who is heir to the biblical promises? The Gospel of Matthew is a Jewish-Christian answer.[1] We find a parallel situation in the Fourth Gospel. With the destruction of the temple, Judaism had to turn, exclusively, to synagogue-centered worship. Jews had to rethink their celebration of the traditional, temple-centered feasts and had to develop their own way of access to God. This is why John 5—10 is dominated by concern with Jewish feasts. More accurately, it is dominated by Jesus' fulfillment of Jewish feasts. In John 5:1, Jesus went to Jerusalem to be present at "a festival of the Jews."

Subsequently, he would be present at Passover (chap. 6), Tabernacles (7:1—10:21), and Dedication (10:22–42). What emerges is that, in practice, Jesus was bringing to fulfillment the purpose of each feast. He is the new focus of worship (see 2:21; 4:21–23).

JESUS AND THE SABBATH (5:1–47)

After the events in Galilee (from Cana to Cana), Jesus went to Jerusalem because "there was a festival of the Jews" (5:1). The feast is unspecified. The key is in verse 9—"Now that day was a sabbath"—Sabbath is the center of this chapter. The vague "a festival of the Jews" is, in some way, a pointer to the issue throughout chapters 5—10.

Healing on a Sabbath (5:1–18)

In Jerusalem, by the pool of Beth-zatha, Jesus happened upon a man who had been disabled for thirty-eight years. He had been by the pool for a long time hoping, in vain, for healing. Jesus healed him. He picked up his sleeping mat and walked away. It was the Sabbath. By carrying a "load," his sleeping mat, the man was infringing a Sabbath rule and was duly challenged by "the Jews." His excuse was that he had been told to do so by the one who had healed him—one whose name he did not know. Later, Jesus met him in the temple. The man went and told "the Jews" that it was Jesus who had healed him. Thereupon "the Jews started persecuting Jesus, because he was doing such things on the sabbath" (v. 16).

Jesus responded, "My Father is still working, and I also am working" (v. 17). Despite Genesis 2:3 ("God rested from all the work that he had done"), Jewish theologians were satisfied that God could never "rest"—he could never cease to be active, even on the Sabbath; otherwise creation would cease to be. Here, Jesus refers to God as Father in a provocative sense. He does this work (healing) on the Sabbath just as his Father works also on the Sabbath. Surely he is usurping a divine prerogative and so "making himself equal to God" (John 5:18)? This charge is likely a Jewish misunderstanding of Johannine Christian claims for Jesus. But John does not make Jesus equal to God (a second God) as is clear in the sequel (vv. 19–30).

Life and Judgment (5:19–30)

The activity of the Son is twofold: giving life and judging. As the Sent One, "the Son can do nothing on his own" (v. 19). Jesus is the apprentice to his Father; all he does he has learned from him (v. 20). As that son–apprentice, the Son can give life as the Father gives life and can judge as the Father judges. To honor the Son, then, is to honor the Father. To hear the word of the Son is to hear the Father and gain eternal life. The one who hears the word of Jesus and trusts in the Father who sent Jesus, has already passed from death to life. The Father is Judge; he has passed on to the Son the authority of judgment. In the Johannine view, however, judgment is auto-judgment—one turns from the light. Verse 30—"I can do nothing on my own"—catches up verse 19—"the Son can do nothing on his own." This underlines the status of the Son as the Sent One. He is the one who wholly represents the Father and speaks fully in his name.

In verses 31–47, the discourse becomes the issue of testimony to Jesus. The question of "witnesses" shifts the language of judging from judgment passed on others to that which others pass on Jesus. Jesus defends himself. He needs witnesses on his behalf—the "two or three witnesses" required by the Law (Deut 19:15). He has formidable witnesses. The Father had borne witness to him through the testimony of the prophet, John the Baptist. The works of Jesus testified on his behalf because they had been wrought by the Father through him. The Scriptures bore witness—scripture is the Word of God. "The Jews" were proud of their knowledge of Scripture; that pride was their undoing. Their disbelief was culpable. They did not "love God," did not respond to God and serve his interests—they were too engrossed in self-interest. Jesus would not be their accuser. Ironically, their accuser would be the very Moses in whom they had placed their hope! If they had really understood their Moses, they would have discerned the continuity of the writings of Moses in the words of Jesus. In the event, he who should have been their advocate will be their prosecutor.

JESUS AND THE PASSOVER (CHAPTER 6)

The Feeding (6:1–15)

All four Gospels carry the story of the multiplication of loaves. Mark (5:32–44; 8:1–10) and Matthew (14:13–21;

15:29–38) have two accounts of a miraculous feeding. There are solid arguments for regarding these two accounts of Matthew and Mark as variant forms of the same incident. Furthermore, it seems best to understand that the Fourth Evangelist (John 6:1–15) drew on an independent tradition quite like that of Mark's and Matthew's second account.

The introductory sentences (vv. 1–3) bring together motifs that belong to the common substance of the gospel tradition: a journey across the lake, the pressure of the crowd, the reputation of Jesus as healer, his withdrawal to the "mountain" with his disciples. In verse 4, we meet a distinctively Johannine trait: "Now the Passover, the festival of the Jews, was near"—note, festival of "the Jews." Passover is the essential background of this chapter. The language of verses 10–12 reflects a eucharistic celebration: Jesus took the loaves, gave thanks, and distributed them. While in the Synoptic Gospels the disciples distributed the bread, John has Jesus himself do it—reminiscent of the Farewell Supper. Only in John is the gathering of fragments given as a command of Jesus: "Gather up the fragments left over, so that nothing may be lost" (v. 12). The use of *synagein*, "gather," and *klasmata*, "fragments," "is peculiar to this Gospel and emphasizes the fact that the fragments are not a remnant but a surplus."[2] In the *Didache*, the same term, *synagein*, is used of gathering for Eucharist. The people observed a "sign" (v. 14) but were not led beyond elementary faith. It seemed to them that Jesus was the prophet-like-Moses (see Deut 18:15–18) of popular expectation. A parallel hope was of a second gift of manna to mark the messianic age (see Bar 29:8). The crowd's further view of him as king was rejected by Jesus as he retired from the scene. He is God's spokesman and true Messiah—but not as perceived by his contemporaries. As Christians, we must be careful not to taint our understanding of Christ with triumphalism.

The incident of walking on the water (vv. 16–21) is closely connected with the feeding of the five thousand also in the Synoptics (Mark 6:45–52; Matt 14:22–23)—evidently, a traditional association. The appearance of Jesus walking on the water is reminiscent of a prerogative of Yahweh (see Job 9:8). Jesus declared "I am" (*ego eimi*), claiming to be much more than the political messiah the crowd had thought him to be. Because of the context, this "I am" may have the resonance of an absolute I AM.

Discourse on the Bread from Heaven (6:25–29)

This discourse is a homily on the text of verse 31—"He gave them bread from heaven to eat." It is interspersed with questions (vv. 25, 28, 30, 42, 52) to which Jesus responds. Verses 25–29 are an introduction. The crowd had seen the "sign" but that had not touched them at any deep level. Jesus accused them of seeking him simply because they had enjoyed a free meal. In verse 27, he began to press his message home in terms of familiar Johannine double meaning: perishable food and the food of eternal life. That abiding food ought to be the object of their striving. There is an implicit contrast with the Law; in Jewish tradition, it was life-giving (see Sir 17:11; 45:5). Jesus offered a better source of life. The crowd wanted to know what they should do to please God ("to perform the works of God" [John 6:28]). What pleases God is to believe in Jesus, the one "whom he has sent." They questioned Jesus' claims. They had seen in him the prophet-like-Moses. Now, they challenged him to provide manna: a sign of the end-time. Jesus' reply was that it was not Moses who *gave* the bread from heaven, it is the Father who *gives* the genuine (*alethinos*), heavenly bread. The true bread from heaven is Jesus. The crowd misunderstood.

Jesus, Bread of Life (6:35–51)

Jesus made a formal declaration: "I am the bread of life" (6:35). This is not a statement of who Jesus is but of what he does: he feeds with life-giving bread. Those given by the Father come to Jesus in faith. He, on his part, welcomes all who come to him and will drive no one away. He acts so because as the Sent One, he responds, without question, to the will of the Father. Not one of those who, given by the Father, come to him, will be lost (see 18:9). All who come to believe in the Son will have life, now and forever.

Up to this point, Jesus had dialoged with "the crowd"; now, at verse 41, the crowd suddenly becomes "the Jews." They "murmured" like the Israelites in the wilderness (see Exod 15:24; 16:2, 7). They challenged his claim to be bread from heaven. They think they know him—son of Joseph. But he had been sent by God from God, and those who believe in him are those whom the Father draws to him. His word is the Word of God. Whoever had listened to him had been taught by the Father. The bread from heaven is revelation of the

Father, in the person and through the words of Jesus. True, Moses had referred to the manna as bread from heaven (see Exod 16:15). Jesus insisted that he is the living bread from heaven. And he elaborated: "The bread that I will give for the life of the world is my flesh" (John 6:51).

My Flesh Is Food Indeed (6:52–59)

If Jesus is both bread and the giver of bread, then what he gives is himself: his flesh and blood. "The Jews," as is to be expected, misunderstood Jesus' promise of the bread that is flesh—his very self. Jesus, in turn, became more explicit: whoever eats the flesh and drinks the blood of him, the Son of Man, has eternal life. "Flesh" points to the human reality of Jesus; "blood" points to the reality of his death. The total gift of himself involves, for Jesus, the breaking of his body and the shedding of his blood. It is the gift of his whole self for the life of the world. Jesus will give his "flesh and blood" at "the hour"—the hour of crucifixion. The death of Jesus is the ultimate revelation of God—who "did not withhold his own Son" (Rom 8:32); who did not shrink from human rejection of himself in the rejection of the Son.

To believe in Jesus is to eat and drink: he is indeed food and drink in that he gives and sustains life. He is living bread; he bestows life on those who accept his revelation of a loving Father; "to eat" Jesus is "to believe" in him. This is a powerful way of stressing the reality of authentic faith and the object of that faith: the Son and his saving death.

> The discourse, from v. 25 down to v. 59, presents Jesus as the true bread from heaven, replacing the former bread from heaven, the manna of the law. The believer must accept the revelation of God that will take place in broken flesh and spilled blood (vv. 53–54)....But at the end of the first century Johannine Christians, and the Christian readers of subsequent centuries, have every right to ask: Where do we encounter this revelation of God in the flesh and blood of the Son of Man? The author's insinuation of eucharistic language into the final section of the discourse provides the answer: one encounters the flesh and blood of Jesus in eucharistic celebration.[3]

Crisis (6:60–71)

It is no surprise that "the Jews" could not accept the word of Jesus. Now we learn that "many of his disciples" would no longer listen to his word (vv. 60–66). They failed to do so because they were operating by human standards—according to "the flesh." Here *sarx*, "flesh," is taken in the sense of the merely human (see 3:6). In contrast, the *sarx* of Jesus is of the Word-made-flesh (1:14) and is life-giving (chap. 6). It is this distinction that explains the seeming contradiction between the positive meaning of "flesh" in verses 51–58 (the flesh of Jesus) and the statement, "the flesh is useless" in verse 63.

What, then, does verse 63 mean? ("It is the spirit that gives life; the flesh is useless. The words that I have spoken to you are spirit and life.") Noteworthy is the reappearance of *pneuma*, "spirit." In the Nicodemus passage (3:1–10), we are told that the realm of "the above" is the sphere of "spirit" and that rebirth into the eternal life of the higher realm is birth "of the Spirit" (3:3–8). And there is the forceful statement, "What is born of the flesh is flesh, and what is born of the Spirit is spirit" (v. 6). Similarly here (6:63), the point is made that only one "born of the Spirit" can accept that Jesus had come from heaven and can receive his revelation. One "born of the flesh," and so open only to the merely human, cannot know him or his teaching. "Because of this many of his disciples turned back and no longer went about with him" (v. 66). This, surely, reflects a Johannine community experience. Some Johannine Christians had left in protest at the high Christology elaborated in the community.

In verse 67, Jesus challenged the Twelve: Will they, too, desert him? Peter assured him that Jesus, and only he, can be the center of their lives: "You have the words of eternal life" (v. 68)—an echo of Jesus' words in verse 63. Peter was sure that Jesus is "the Holy One of God." The Twelve had come "to believe and know" (v. 69): they had attained full Johannine faith. It was at a price. The chapter ends on a somber note (vv. 70–71): Jesus, Bread of Life—the life-giver—will be brought to death by unbelief and betrayal.

JESUS AND TABERNACLES (7:1—10:21)

The Feast of Tabernacles is the background for 7:1—10:21. The Hebrew *sukkot* is variously translated: Tabernacles, Booths, Tents, Shelters. It was celebrated in autumn, in the seventh month (September–October). It was originally a seven-day festival to which an eighth day was added. Of the annual pilgrim feasts, this was the best attended. Josephus referred to it as "the holiest and greatest of Hebrew feasts." Two of its ceremonies are of immediate relevance here: water libation and light. Each morning, a procession, led by priests, brought water from the pool of Siloam. It was taken to the temple and poured over the altar. Jewish tradition linked the Messiah with the gift of water. Four menorahs (the seven-branched lampstands) were set up in the center of the court of the women. They lighted up the night.

At the Feast (7:1–36)

Opposition to Jesus had hardened and had begun to mobilize. Jesus decided to remain in Galilee for some time; "the Jews" were planning to kill him if he moved into Judea. His brothers (last mentioned at 2:12) urged him to go with them to Jerusalem for the Feast of Tabernacles where he might display his works. He told them to go by themselves; his hour for "going up" was not yet. Later he did, quietly, go to Jerusalem. "The Jews" had sought him and were disappointed that he had not shown up. "Where is he?" He was being discussed. Some of the people were on Jesus' side; others thought he was a heretic. This is a reflection of debates over Jesus between Johannine Christians and their opponents.

Halfway through the week-long feast, Jesus began to teach openly in the temple. There was surprise on the part of "the Jews": Where did he get his theological learning? The basic issue was one of authority: Is God revealed in Jewish tradition or in Jesus' teaching? Jesus responded that he had his teaching from him who had sent him. People of good will would readily discern the source of his teaching. He accused "the Jews" of self-interest and of seeking to kill him. They had criticized Jesus for healing on the Sabbath (see 5:2–18). They themselves had no problem with performing circumcision on the Sabbath. What, then, was wrong with Jesus' healing "a man's whole body" (v. 23)?

Some of the people were surprised that Jesus had appeared openly; they knew that "the Jews" were seeking to kill him. Perhaps the authorities had come to accept that Jesus was the Messiah after all? On the other hand, the Messiah would remain hidden until his spectacular appearance (a popular notion). But all knew that Jesus was from Nazareth. Johannine irony: they do not know the true provenance of Jesus. He informed them that he was from the one who had sent him—the one they did not know. "The Jews" understood that he was, again, referring to his Father. They would have arrested him, but it was not yet his "hour." Some did believe that Jesus was the Messiah. Their belief fell short of Johannine faith (vv. 25–31). The priests and Pharisees had not given in; they sent temple police to arrest him. Jesus told his opponents that he would soon return to him who had sent him. They would seek him in vain, for they could not follow him. They surmised the following: Was he going to the diaspora, outside their control? (vv. 32–36).

On the Last Day of the Feast (7:37—8:59)

The last day of the festival was the eighth. The water and light ceremonies had ended on the previous seventh day. Jesus now proclaimed that he was the giver of water (vv. 37–38) and light of the world (8:12). This eighth day is, truly, "the great day" (7:37).

Jesus made a solemn proclamation:

> Let anyone who is thirsty come to me, and let the one who believes in me drink. As the scripture has said, "Out of his heart shall flow rivers of living water." (vv. 37–38) (Author's translation)

In Ezekiel 47:1–12, life-giving waters flowed from the temple. Jesus declared that life-giving water flowed from him; his person is now the source of living water. He spoke of the Spirit, the powerful presence of God. "For as yet there was no Spirit" (v. 39): the Spirit would not be until Jesus had been "glorified." The risen Christ will give the Spirit (see 20:22). Only when manifested ("glorified") on the cross will he be wholly the dispenser of God's power (vv. 37–39).

Questions about Jesus' identity persisted. The crowd was divided. Some, though they had not understood, were impressed: here was the prophet-like-Moses—perhaps even the Messiah! Others objected that the Messiah would come from Bethlehem, village of David. Jesus was a Galilean. The origin of Jesus had them well and truly puzzled (vv. 40–41). The authorities had sent temple police to arrest Jesus (v. 32).

These returned to the chief priests and Pharisees empty-handed. When asked why they had failed to arrest him, they could only answer that never had they heard anyone speak as Jesus had spoken. The annoyed Pharisees retorted that the authorities were not so gullible; only the accursed rabble who knew nothing of the Law could be deceived. Nicodemus protested: Surely the Law expects us to grant a fair hearing before we condemn? He got short shrift. With heavy sarcasm, he was asked, Are you a Galilean too? You are supposed to know your scripture; then you must know that prophets do not come from Galilee! One thing had become clear: Jesus' enemies might not know what to make of him, but they were grimly set on getting rid of him (vv. 45–52).

The Light of the World (8:12–30)

The ceremony of light had concluded. On this last day of Tabernacles, Jesus declared, "I am the light of the world" (v.12). As light of the world (1:9), his coming had divided humanity into those who "come to the light" and those whose evil deeds led them to choose darkness (3:19–21). Jesus had fulfilled the light ceremonies of Tabernacles as he had previously brought to fulfillment its water ritual. He was the light: whoever would follow him would walk in the light of life. The Pharisees objected that his self-witness was not valid; that, in fact, he lied. Jesus emphatically asserted that his testimony was true and valid. He knew whence he came and where he was going. They did not know and were in no position to pass judgment on him. They judged by human standards, and condemned him. He was not in the business of condemning anyone. To the question, "Where is your Father?" he retorted that if they knew him, they would know the Father. As it was, they knew neither Son nor Father. He continued to teach openly and was not arrested "because his hour had not yet come" (vv. 12–20).

Jesus told his opponents that he was going where they could not come (see 7:33–36). They wondered aloud whether he intended to commit suicide! He and they belonged to two different worlds. He had come into their world to empower them to be begotten from above. To attain that eternal life, they must believe Jesus' assertion: I AM (*ego eimi*). They must believe that he possessed the life-giving power of the Father. Throughout Second Isaiah (see 41:4; 43:10, 13; 45:18; 46:4; 48:12), the expression "I am" is used to present Yahweh as the unique God of Israel, and as the only God. By using the same formula, Jesus makes the unique claim to be the presence of God to humankind. He drove the matter home: "When you have lifted up the Son of Man, then you will realize that I AM" (v. 28 ISV). They may crucify him ("lift up"); indeed, they will. But that "lifting up" will be his revelation of God. It is because he is one with the Father—the Sent One who wholly represents the Father—that Jesus can speak his I AM. Jesus is the unique revelation of God (vv. 21–30).

Jesus went on to tell "the Jews" that the truth would set them free—meaning that he was truth, embodying the Father's saving purpose. They retorted that they stood in no need of being set free: they were free children of Abraham. Jesus rejoined that they were slaves, slaves of sin. As for being children of Abraham, why did they want to kill him? That was not to act as Abraham's children. In fact, they were doing the work of their father. They protested, "God is our father!" Jesus replied that, if it were so, they would love him, the Son. But, "you are from your father the devil" (v. 44). They prove it because they turn from the truth and embrace lies. Could any of them convict Jesus of sin, of turning from God's purpose? If they were from God, they would have hearkened to the Word of God that he had spoken. In the Johannine view, people have to be "from God" or "not from God" (vv. 31–47).

"The Jews" counterattacked: Jesus is "a Samaritan," and has a "demon." A lively dialogue ensued. He retorted, "I do not have a demon; but I honor my Father, and you dishonor me. Yet I do not seek my own glory; there is one who seeks it and he is the judge. Very truly, I tell you, whoever keeps my word will never see death" (vv. 49–51). They shot back, "Now we know that you have a demon. Abraham died, and so did the prophets; yet you say, 'Whoever keeps my word will never taste death.' Are you greater than our father Abraham, who died?...Who do you claim to be?" Jesus answered, "Your ancestor Abraham rejoiced that he would see my day [the age to come had been revealed to him by God]; he saw it and was glad." They retorted, "You are not yet fifty years old, and have you seen Abraham?" Jesus fired his parting shot: "Very truly, I tell you, before Abraham was, I AM"—the one who bears God's name and wields his power. The claim was blasphemy to them. They attempted to stone him, but he left the temple and slipped away. The rift was complete (vv. 48–59).

EXCURSUS: THE WOMAN TAKEN IN ADULTERY (8:1–11)

While, in form and style, this passage—the woman taken in adultery—closely resembles the Synoptic tradition, it is not in context in the Fourth Gospel. It is more in the style of Luke and seems to have been inserted in John because of the reference in 7:51 to judgment according to the Law.

The purpose of the scribes and Pharisees in bringing the adulteress to Jesus was to entrap him. If he pardoned her, he could be accused of encouraging people to infringe the Law of Moses that prescribed death by stoning for such conduct (see Lev 20:10; Deut 13:9–10). In fact, as the Wisdom literature makes clear, that grim prescription had long been a dead letter, but the law could still be invoked as a challenge to Jesus. On the other hand, if he would agree that she should be stoned to death, he would lose his name for mercy. Jesus deftly turned the challenge: let the woman's accusers look to their own sins! He will not be judge. Although the Father had given full authority to his Son to pass judgment (John 5:22), Jesus really judges no one (8:15). His message is of mercy and forgiveness.

The story ends with the quiet scene of reconciliation between Jesus and the woman. The accusers had gone; Jesus alone remained to proclaim to her God's mercy. Augustine comments, *relicti sunt duo—misera et misericordia*: "two stood there alone—wretchedness and mercy."

HEALING OF A MAN BORN BLIND (CHAPTER 9)

Like the episode of the Samaritan woman (chap. 4), this splendid story is, too, a lesson on growth in faith. The miracle of the granting of sight to a blind man is a "sign." Jesus thereby reveals that he is "the light of the world" (v. 5)—still the Tabernacles setting. In giving physical sight, Jesus demonstrated that by his teaching, life, and personal presence, he was the source of the spiritual vision we call "believing." The whole account reads like a picturesque, symbolic presentation of the manner in which one comes to believe in Jesus as "Lord." Healed quickly of his physical disability, the man was the subject of a gradual illumination ("the man called Jesus," " a prophet," "a man from God") until, finally, he came to faith: "Lord, I believe" (v. 38).

An Old Testament view (firmly endorsed by Job's theologian "comforters") saw a necessary link between affliction and sin; Jesus rejected any such necessary connection (vv. 1–3). The man was bidden to wash in the pool of Siloam (Tabernacles association)—"which means Sent." This is a play on the name *Siloam*; in the context, reference is to "the One Sent." He "came back able to see" (v. 7). Yet, the cure was really achieved not by the waters of Siloam but by the Sent One. His neighbors and those who recognized the beggar wanted to know how it happened that he was now sighted. He told them that the one who had healed him was "the man called Jesus" (v. 11). It happened to be a Sabbath. The Pharisees considered Jesus' making of the paste he spread on the patient's eyes to be "work" and so an infringement of Sabbath observance (vv. 6–7, 14). Some immediately concluded that Jesus, as one who did not honor the Sabbath, could not be from God. Others were not so sure: could a sinner give sight to the blind? As often in John, a "division" (*schisma*) occurred. The man who earlier had referred to "the man called Jesus" now stated his deeper conviction; "He is a prophet" (vv. 1–17).

The Pharisees—here "the Jews"—called the parents to account. They acknowledged that their son had been born blind. They have no idea how it is he now sees. And they will not get involved. The fear of the parents (v. 22) and the de facto expulsion of their son (v. 34) reflect a time when one could no longer profess faith in Jesus Christ and remain within the community of Israel. At first, Jewish Christians had been tolerated by their fellow Jews. In the Johannine situation, the matter was exacerbated by the distinctive Johannine Christology (vv. 18–23).

"The Jews" then attempted to proclaim Jesus a sinner and questioned the man again. They reviled him for his claim that Jesus is from God. They adjured the man: "Give glory to God" (v. 24)—a formula used when one is to confess one's guilt. He insisted that Jesus had healed his blindness—scarcely the deed of a sinner (it could only have been God's achievement, through Jesus). As they pressed their questioning, he observed, sarcastically, that they seemed so interested in Jesus that they must be thinking of becoming his disciples! Angrily, they retorted, "We are disciples of Moses. We know that God has spoken to Moses, but as for this man, we do not know where he comes from" (vv. 28–29). This exchange set the man among the "disciples of Jesus" and "the Jews" as "disciples of Moses"—again, a later conflict situation between the Christian community and the synagogue. The man would not be browbeaten: "You do not know where he comes from, and yet he opened my eyes....Never since the world began has it been heard that anyone opened the eyes of a person born blind. If this man were not from God, he could do nothing" (vv. 30, 32–33). The man's faith grew as he stoutly defended Jesus. He became more and more convinced that Jesus was from God (the Sent One). Sadly, while the blind man opened more and more to the light, the Pharisees, though physically sighted, were spiritually blind. The man was driven from the synagogue. It was the experience of Johannine Christians who had been similarly expelled (vv. 24–34).

The man was ready for a further step on his faith journey. Jesus encountered him and issued the challenge: "Do you believe in the Son of Man?" (v. 35). With charming directness he replied, "Who is he, sir? Tell me, so that I may believe in him" (v. 36). Convinced that he had seen the Son and had heard his word, he made his profession: "Lord, I believe!" (v. 38) and fell on his knees in acknowledgment of the God-sent bringer of salvation. He had advanced from his Jewish belief (vv. 31–33) to Christian faith. Yet, there remain those who would not believe (vv. 39–41). The blind man could not "see" in the manner of the Pharisees with their vaunted knowledge of the Law and of the ways of God, but he was open and could come to faith. Those who could "see" were blinkered by that puny light that held their gaze and could not perceive the Light of the World (vv. 35–41).

JESUS, GOOD SHEPHERD (10:1–21)

Against the background of Ezekiel 34, Jesus presented himself as the "shepherd" of God's flock and the "door" of access to God. In a Palestinian setting, the sheepfold was a courtyard or a walled enclosure in a field. At night, the sheep of various shepherds were gathered within. There was a proper manner of approaching sheep herded in a sheepfold: through the gate opened by the keeper. Any other mode of entry was the conduct of a thief. Then there is the shepherd. He knows his sheep by name; when he calls them, they follow him confidently. They will not follow a stranger; they do not recognize his voice. The parabolic form wears thin as Jesus reveals his own part in the picture. It is because the parable is really about him that the same person can fill the role of shepherd and also of gate giving access to the fold. The Lord not only gives and sustains life but is also the way, or means of entry, into life. As the Good Shepherd, Jesus contrasted himself with the Pharisees who had just expelled from the synagogue the man born blind (9:34). Jesus "leads out" and "goes ahead of" his sheep as their leader and guides them to the pasturage of his word. And he calls each "by name"—there is a close personal relationship between the Christian and Christ.

Jesus also described himself as the gate of the sheepfold; he is the way of life (see 14:6). In and through him alone do

Christians enter into "life"—a gift bestowed with lavish generosity. Here, there is the same loving care as before and the same intimate familiarity—they "come in and go out" as they please (10:9). While Jesus spoke of himself as shepherd and way, the passage must be a challenge to all who hold pastoral responsibility. They will do well to contemplate the picture of caring vigilance and patient love that the good shepherd presents, and mark his respect for the freedom of his disciples (vv. 1–10).

Jesus declared himself to be the Good (or ideal) Shepherd. Again, Ezekiel 34 is the background. God promises his people, in the first place, that he would become their shepherd, and then that he would choose a shepherd for them in the messianic age. Jesus' assertion that he is the Good Shepherd indicates that this age has come, and that he is that promised shepherd. He is a shepherd so very different from those castigated by Ezekiel: "You have not strengthened the weak, you have not healed the sick, you have not bound up the injured, you have not brought back the strayed, you have not sought the lost, but with force and harshness you have ruled them" (Ezek 34:4). On every point, he stood in sharp contrast.

The second characteristic of the true Shepherd is that he knows his sheep intimately and that they know him. In John, the mutual knowledge of Jesus and those who belong to him is an extension of the mutual knowledge of Father and Son (see John 17:26–27). Knowing Jesus and the Father is being of one mind and heart with them. But the shepherd concern of Jesus reached out to other sheep—the Gentiles—to bring them also into the fold of eternal life. Jesus declared that the Father loved him because he was prepared to sacrifice life itself in faithfulness to the task entrusted to him. Because he was so fully one with the Father, source of life and life-giver, he had power not only to lay down his life, but power to take it up again. "I have received this command from my Father"; as always in John, it is the Father who initiates activity (10:11–18).

"The Jews" did not know what to make of Jesus' words—again, a "division." Some declared flatly, "He…is out of his mind." Others observed more thoughtfully, "These are not the words of one who has a demon. Can a demon open the eyes of the blind?" (vv. 19–21). The question of who Jesus is will not go away.

JESUS AND DEDICATION (10:22–42)

The origin of the Feast of Dedication (*Hanukkah*) is described in 1 Maccabees 4:36–59: purification of the temple on the twenty-fifth Kislev (December), 164 BCE, after Judas Maccabeus's successful campaign to liberate Jerusalem. The feast lasted eight days and was marked by an atmosphere of rejoicing. The rituals of Hanukkah were similar to those of Tabernacles.

The passage John 10:22–39, in the setting of Dedication, presents Jesus as Messiah and Son of God. The debates of Tabernacles continue. The Messiah question is raised in verse 24, "If you are the Messiah, tell us plainly." Jesus responded by pointing to the works he was doing.

Verses 26–27 recall 10:1–21, the faithful sheep know the voice of their shepherd. Verse 28 recalls the wolves that snatch the sheep when the hireling fails to protect the flock (see 10:12). Jesus is the true Shepherd and no one will snatch from his care the sheep that the Father has given him. Observe the correspondence of verses 28 and 29: "No one will snatch them out of my hand"; "no one can snatch it out of the Father's hand." What comfort for the sheep! "The Father and I are one" (v. 30): the Father and Jesus share oneness of purpose. Consequently, Jesus is the visible presence of God (vv. 22–30).

"The Jews" accused Jesus of "blasphemy," usurpation of divine status and honor. They spelled out their charge: "You, though only a human being, are making yourself God" (v. 33). They had misunderstood Jesus' words in verse 30 ("the Father and I are one") as a claim to be God (see 19:7). In his reply (vv. 34–35), Jesus followed a Jewish debating technique. Psalm 82:6 states, "I say, 'You are gods, children of the Most High, all of you.'" The psalm castigates unjust judges. They are called "gods" because of their quasi-divine function (judgment belongs to God; see Deut 1:17). Jesus' argument runs: First, if Scripture can refer to human beings as "gods," why do "the Jews" object when the term is applied to Jesus? Second, the judges were called "gods" because they were agents of God. A fortiori, Jesus, as consecrated agent of the Father, deserves to be called "god." In short, if those who speak in God's name are "gods," why not Jesus who does the work of God? In John 10:36, "I am God's Son" is an explanation of the declaration "the Father and I are one" (v. 30):

the Father had sent Jesus and had given him a unique task. There is a further explanation in verse 38—"the Father is in me and I am in the Father": Father and Son, though distinct, are one in a mutual sharing of life. The debate that started at Tabernacles and ended at Dedication closed on a tragic note (v. 39). There is no longer any hope that "the Jews" would listen to Jesus (vv. 31–39).

All was not lost. Jesus went across the Jordan to where John the Baptist had begun his mission. The move reminded some that what John had said of Jesus had turned out to be true. These believed in him. Francis Moloney observes that this fulfillment of Jewish feasts needs to be carefully assessed. A proper understanding will aid, not confuse, Jewish-Christian dialogue.

> The gospel does not attempt to denigrate the established ways of remembering and rendering present God's saving action among the people of Israel. The account of Jesus' presence at their feasts—Sabbath, Passover, Tabernacles, and Dedication—affirm that the former order has been perfected, not destroyed. The crucial difference between the two orders is the person of Jesus Christ. The conflict between Jesus and "the Jews," as it is reported in these stories, is not a conflict between Jesus and Israel but rather a conflict between some from Israel who had definitively decided that Jesus was or was not the Christ; anyone who confessed he was must be put out of the synagogue (cf. 9:22). As Jesus and "the Jews" are on a collision course, so

> are "the Jews" and the Johannine Christians, but the latter are proud to look back upon their Jewish heritage, to see in their former festive celebrations of God in Israel the signs and shadows of the presence of Jesus among them.[4]

SUMMARY

Jesus had spoken of his body as a new temple (2:19–21) and had told the Samaritan woman, "the hour is coming... when the true worshippers will worship the Father in spirit and truth" (4:23). Now, in chapters 5—10, he is the one who brings to fulfillment the Sabbath and the great feasts of Israel. He heals on a Sabbath because his Father works good even on the Sabbath. He does the divine works of giving life and of judging. These works, and the Father himself, are his authenticating witness.

A feeding of five thousand led to a discourse on heavenly bread, bread of life. Jesus is the bread of life, fulfilling the promise of the manna. He is the true bread given by the Father: the bread of revelation of the Father. He is "bread" of flesh and blood: flesh as truly human, blood as one who died. His gift was of himself for the life of the world. Faith in him is the "eating" and "drinking" of his "flesh and blood." He gives and sustains life. Not all Johannine Christians could accept the high Christology behind these assertions.

At Tabernacles, Jesus emerged as the source of the "water of life." As such, he is giver of the Spirit. He is the "I AM": the presence of God, endowed with the life-giving power of the Father. His full revelation of the Father is in his being "lifted up." The healing of the blind man was a "sign": Jesus is light of the world. The man had walked a journey of faith, to the point where he professed, "Lord, I believe"—and worshipped.

Jesus is the Good Shepherd who knows his sheep, who lovingly cares for them, who respects their freedom. He is the Gateway to Life. His sheep hear his voice and follow. No one will snatch them out of his hand. He is, truly, God's Son who does the work of his Father. The Father is the God of salvation. Father and Son are at one in this purpose.

Notes

1. Wilfrid J. Harrington, *Reading Matthew for the First Time* (Mahwah, NJ: Paulist Press, 2014), 5–9.

2. Michael Mullins, *The Gospel of John. A Commentary* (Dublin: Columba Press, 2003), 188.

3. Francis J. Moloney, *The Gospel of John* (Collegeville, MN: Liturgical Press, 1998), 223.

4. Ibid., 318f.

CHAPTER 4

Toward the Hour

FROM DEATH TO LIFE (11:1–54)

Jesus' raising of Lazarus is a "sign," the most poignant sign of his life-giving mission. It is an illustration of his claim to be the resurrection and the life (11:25–26) and an indication that the "last day" has dawned: "Very truly, I tell you, the hour is coming, and is now here, when the dead will hear the voice of the Son of God, and those who hear will live" (5:25). As in the episode of Jesus' healing of the man born blind (chap. 9), the Evangelist's intention is to give a vivid pictorial presentation of the effect of believing in Jesus. There he appeared as light of the world; here he appears as life of the world. The Evangelist does not want our attention to be arrested by the wonderful fact that Jesus had performed the impossible in bringing a man back to life. He wants us to see in Jesus the source of life: he is the life-giving Word of God incarnate (1:4, 14). The life in question is not earthly life. The resuscitation of Lazarus is but a pointer to the life that Jesus provides.

We must appreciate that the resurrection that Jesus promises, here and now, to those who believe in him is to be understood no more literally than the "resurrection" of Ezekiel 37. What Jesus proclaims is that the new life of the new covenant has been given to the world in him. It is available to all who believe in him, who rely on him, and who trust in him, building their lives on his. This new life is not just a future hope. It is a present reality that physical death, despite its appearance of finality, will not negate. It is not a life merely juxtaposed to ordinary human existence, but ordinary human existence lived in a new manner, in knowledge of the one true God who has revealed himself and his plan for humankind in his Son: "And this is eternal life, that they may know you, the only true God, and Jesus Christ whom you have sent" (John 17:3). It is knowledge of God as Father, the realization that love is at the heart of reality, which changes existence into life.

The Raising of Lazarus (11:1–53)

Luke also notes the sisters, Martha and Mary, as friends of Jesus (he does not mention Lazarus) (see 10:38–42). Now, in John, their brother, Lazarus, is gravely ill and the sisters send word to Jesus. Their discreet invitation, "Lord, he whom you love is ill" is reminiscent of 2:3—"they have no wine." Jesus declared that the illness would lead to his "glorification": the revelation of God's power in the Son. His statement, "this illness does not lead to death," means that the death of Lazarus will not be the last word. Jesus stayed where he was for two days; his actions can never be measured by human standards (see 7:8). Then he set out for Bethany, brushing aside the remonstrances of his disciples who reminded him that last time in Jerusalem, "the Jews" had attempted to stone him (10:31). His reason for going to Bethany was a response to God's design. He told his disciples bluntly that Lazarus was dead. He was "glad" for their sake because they would receive a new stimulus for their faith. Thomas misunderstood; Jesus sought their belief, not their death. Jesus knew that he would call Lazarus to life, though his life-giving would cost him his own life (11:1–16).

On arrival at Bethany, he found that Lazarus had been buried four days earlier. When she was told that he had reached the village, Martha came to meet him; Mary stayed at home. The sisters display the same temperaments as in Luke 10:38–41, and here, as there, Mary is the special one. Martha has an open-ended faith: "Even now I know that God will give you whatever you ask of him" (John 11:22). Jesus declared himself to be the resurrection and the life. One who believes in him will have life beyond death—resurrection life. In response, Martha protested her belief in Jesus—as "Messiah, Son of God, the one coming into the world" (v. 27). It seems a fulsome declaration. Yet, by John's standards, her profession remained at the level of traditional messianic expectation.[1]

Martha went to her sister. Her words, "the Teacher…is calling for you," (v. 28) recall 10:3: here was the Good Shepherd (see 20:16). Mary responded to the call; she saw Jesus and knelt at his feet. She acknowledged his presence and displayed unconditional trust in him. And then, in a peculiar form of Johannine irony, she promptly proceeded to disappoint Jesus.

Verse 33 attests a startling demonstration of emotion by Jesus. Ostensibly, he wept in bitter grief over the death of a friend. Such raw emotion is unexpected of the Johannine Jesus and, in this instance, even more so from a Jesus who knew full well that it was a moment of his "glorification." John writes that Jesus was "greatly disturbed in spirit and deeply moved." This is strong language. It suggests not conventional grief but bitter disappointment. A Mary who had shown her appreciation of the true nature of Jesus and of what he was about, now joins "the Jews" (vv. 31–36) in their mourning of the dead and in their estimation of the merely human tears of Jesus. John is precise. Jesus wept (*dakruo*); Mary cried (*klaio*). Jesus was not mourning. He grieved, not over Lazarus (who would be restored to life) but over Mary's "relapse."[2]

Jesus had been invited to "come and see" where Lazarus had been buried (v. 34). In the event, Jesus was not shown to the tomb; he came to the place. As it will be throughout the passion, already at this approach to "the hour," Jesus is in charge as he calmly carries through God's purpose. They would "see the glory of God." Jesus' prayer was a proclamation to those present that the stupendous event about to take place was the deed of the Father. The Father's life-giving power was his as the Sent One. The details of verse 44 are deliberately designed to turn the reader's attention to another tomb (19:40–41) and to other grave clothes (20:5–7). The raising of Lazarus does point to him who is resurrection and life (vv. 38–44).

If some of "the Jews" were prepared to acknowledge Jesus, the "chief priests and Pharisees" most definitely were not. They agreed that they could not permit him to go on working signs. Sooner or later, there would be provocation and the Romans would surely intervene. They would destroy the temple and the very nation. Here is manifest awareness of the Jewish war of 65–70 CE. Caiaphas, high priest that fateful year, spoke up: "It is better for you to have one man die for the people than to have the whole nation destroyed" (v. 50). Here, we certainly have cynical political opportunism—but also much more than that. Caiaphas was, unawares, making a prophetic pronouncement: Jesus was to die for the salvation of the nation and of the world. The death of Jesus would "gather into one the dispersed children of God" (v. 52). One is reminded of 1 John 2:2: "He is the atoning sacrifice for our sins, and not for ours only but also for the sins of the whole world." Jesus withdrew from the city. He went into the wilderness, poised for "the hour" (vv. 45–54).

THE HOUR HAS COME (11:55—12:36)

Six days before Passover, Jesus left his wilderness retreat and came again to Bethany, to the home of Lazarus and his sisters. Martha, the practical hostess, served a meal. The contrast between the women persists, as in Luke 10:38–42. Mary, the romantic one, came with a flask of expensive ointment. She anointed Jesus' feet and wiped them off with her long hair. The perfume filled the house, the perfume of Mary's love. Judas protested the waste. The name of Judas, notoriously familiar to the readers as the betrayer, already signals the passion of Jesus. An unsavory feature is the demonization of Judas, here, as "a thief."

The Mary who had so disappointed Jesus (11:33) is wholly rehabilitated. Now she does respond to the voice of the Good Shepherd (10:27) and, anticipating the burial of Jesus, she becomes the first to understand the significance of his death. Many had come from Jerusalem, not only to meet Jesus, but to see Lazarus, a nine days' wonder indeed. The chief priests were thinking of doing away with him also; people were believing in Jesus because of Lazarus (11:55—12:10).

To Jerusalem (12:12–36)

This visit of Jesus to Jerusalem was unlike his former visits—2:12–22; 5:1; 7:10. Here his approach to the city is described as a "coming," not as a "going up." He received an enthusiastic reception. A "great crowd" met him with cries of "Hosanna!" and waving branches of palm. The quotation in verse 13 is directly from Psalm 118:25–26. The reference is messianic, as in verse 15 (see Zech 9:9). The phrase "the one who comes in the name of the Lord" applies perfectly to Jesus, who comes in the name of and with the power of God.

If there were overtones of nationalistic enthusiasm in the festive welcome, Jesus moved quickly to defuse the situation. "Jesus found a young donkey and sat on it" (v. 14); he did not come as a temporal ruler in worldly pomp. Notably, where the text of Zechariah 9:9 begins "Rejoice greatly," the Johannine text substitutes "Do not be afraid!" The manner of entry of this humble king anticipates Jesus' declaration to

Pilate: "My kingdom is not from this world" (John 18:36). At the time, the disciples were unable to grasp the significance of this messianic entry. Later, after the death of Jesus, they perceived its meaning. The story of the raising of Lazarus was rippling through the enthusiastic crowd. Exasperated Pharisees explained petulantly: "You see, you can do nothing. Look, the world has gone after him!" (12:19). They spoke more truly than they could ever imagine.

Some God-fearers, Gentiles strongly attracted to Judaism, had come to Jerusalem for Passover. Through Philip (a Greek name—a Greek-speaker), they asked to speak with Jesus. Surprisingly, instead of complying with the request, Jesus stated a fundamental truth to guide all his followers: "Unless a grain of wheat falls into the earth and dies, it remains just a single grain; but if it dies, it bears much fruit" (v. 24). Following Christ involves evaluating one's earthly life and possessions, and the readiness to yield everything for his service.

The time for Jesus' passion has come. He fears it, yet longs for it. He is troubled. Should he ask the Father to save him from the cross? No! He sets his mind to fulfill this task: "It is for this reason that I have come to this hour" (v. 27). Further, he is sure that in this hour of crisis and suffering, he will be glorified. Here, in this attitude of Jesus to his coming passion, we find a parallel with Hebrews 5:7–9. The high priest experiences the pain of obedience, yet accepts it totally, and through it is fulfilled.

Jesus explained more fully in John 12:32–33 the relation between his sacrificial death and the life of humankind. The death of Jesus would be his most eloquent sermon: the ultimate revelation of the Father. His death was also judgment on the unbelieving world. It was a death-blow to evil. The "ruler of the world" is personification of all the opposition of the *archontes,* the "rulers," to Jesus throughout the ministry and to the cross. His death was firmly positive: "And I, when I am lifted up from the earth, will draw all people to myself" (12:32). This "lifting up," in the language of the Fourth Gospel, is both the physical posture of crucifixion (see 3:14, "as Moses lifted up the serpent in the wilderness") and the divine act by which Jesus was glorified, on account of his obedient death. Just as he was lifted up in torment by sinful men (and it was men, not women, who brought about the death of Jesus), even so was he raised in immortal triumph, by the Father, to be Savior of all.

"And I, when I am lifted up from the earth, will draw all people to myself." Jesus was doing much more than indicating the manner of his death. The crowd did not catch his meaning. He issued a final warning. He pleaded, "Walk while you have the light, so that the darkness may not overtake you" (12:35). In other words, *turn to the light. Believe in me while you still have time. I have always spoken in the name of the Father who sent me. The Father is greater than I. Nevertheless, to hear me is to hear the Father, your God. To believe in me is to put your faith in him.*

Jesus left them. His mission was ended. Or, was it only beginning? His hour had come (vv. 12–36).

The Evangelist's Comment (12:37–50)

The text of Isaiah 56:9–10 is invoked in three New Testament settings: to explain the negative reaction to the parables of Jesus (Mark 4:10–12, Luke 8:9–10), to his "signs" (John 12:37–41), and to Paul's ministry to Jews (Acts 28:25–27). In its Isaian context, the declaration of Isaiah 6:9–10 is a forceful and paradoxical proclamation of what, inevitably, is going to happen: the Prophet's message will not be heeded. Early Christian thinkers tended to account for the rejection of the message of Jesus by asserting that such, strangely, was the will of God. There were always those who did not hearken. Yet, some even of the "authorities" came to believe in Jesus. Like Nicodemus, they remained crypto-disciples. "They loved human glory more than the glory that comes from God" (John 12:43). The Johannine author is unrelenting in his Two Ways theology (see Deut 30:15–20). He will find scope for dramatic development in the Roman trial of Jesus (vv. 37–50).

In verses 44–50, the Evangelist has Jesus, who had already left the stage (12:36), cry out his final word. He presents himself as the Sent One. As God's agent, he is the one in whom God is fully present. As the agent of his Father, he is not in the business of judgment. This Savior God sent his Son into the world to save that world. Salvation is his one concern. As obedient Son/Agent, Jesus obeys wholly the One who sent him. He obeys a commandment. What a glorious commandment: "I know that his commandment is eternal life" (v. 50).

In the Fourth Gospel, the raising of Lazarus brought the opposition to Jesus to its climax. For Jesus, himself, it was his final sign. It revealed him as the resurrection and the life. The sisters, Martha and Mary, illustrate the recurring Johannine theme of coming to faith. Mary responded to the call of the

Good Shepherd, then wavered, but finally came to full faith by her anointing of Jesus, her recognition of the significance of his death. Jesus made his messianic entry into Jerusalem in his own fashion. It was enough to exasperate "the Jews"—the world had gone after him. The hour had come, the hour of the death of the "grain of wheat." Lifted up, he would draw all people to himself.

Notes

1. Others would evaluate differently. "Martha's response is the most fully developed confession of faith in the Fourth Gospel. She recognizes in Jesus the Christ (Messiah), the Son of God...the one sent into the world by the Father." Sandra M. Schneiders, "Death in the Community of Eternal Life," *Interpretation* 41 (1987): 52–54; Schneiders, *Written That You May Believe: Encountering Jesus in the Fourth Gospel* (New York: Crossroad, 1999), 158.

2. Francis J. Moloney, *The Gospel of John* (Collegeville, MN: Liturgical Press, 1998), 330–31. In a different vein, Schneiders, *Written That You May Believe*, 159, notes that a Jesus here "greatly disturbed in spirit and deeply moved" (11: 33) will, when confronted with the reality of his own death, confess: "Now my soul is troubled" (12:27). She adds, "Jesus' tears are an honest sharing in Mary's grief and perhaps her anger at death, the enemy of all life. Jesus, in his most fully human moment in the Fourth Gospel, legitimates human agony in the face of death, an agony he will feel for himself as he shrinks from the passion in chapter 12. This episode roots the spirituality of the community in the realism of human experience. Christian faith is neither Gnosticism nor stoicism. Death is real and so is the suffering it causes. Faith is not compatible with despair, but it is no stranger to tears." The problem remains that Jesus is grieving the death of Lazarus—just as he is about to raise him to life!

CHAPTER 5

Meal and Discourse

The hour had come. Before departing, Jesus would tell his disciples, in a manner they could never forget, how utterly he loved them. Jesus knew that he was about to give the supreme manifestation (see 15:13) of his abiding love for his disciples. He himself demonstrates clearly the meaning of what he did; the act of humble service he now rendered. His symbolic act of foot washing characterized his imminent suffering and death as a work of service. The opening words, "Having loved his own who were in the world, he loved them to the end" (13:1) are a caption for all that is to come in chapters 13—17, the demonstration of Jesus' love for his own (*eis telos*)—unconditional and without measure. Very soon, he will declare that this love transcends death. Now he gives them a dramatic example of loving service.

FRIENDSHIP (CHAPTER 13)

Service is something one person does for another for the good of the other. One lays aside one's own good. The ultimate expression is to lay down one's very life—"It is a far, far better thing I do than I have ever done."[1] Sandra Schneiders offers a careful analysis of service, noting that, with one exception, service involves inequality. In the first place, the obvious inequality between master and servant is reinforced by the service of the latter. Second, even the service of a mother rendered to her child, though inspired by love, still involves inequality. The third model, at its finest, avoids the condition of inequality.[2]

Friendship is the one human relationship based on equality. In perfect friendship, which is rare indeed, the good of each is truly the other's good and so, in seeking the good of the friend, one's own good is achieved. But this self-fulfillment involves no subversive seeking of self; it is simply the by-product of the friend's happiness. This is why service rendered between friends is never exacted and creates no debts, demands no return but evokes reciprocity, and never degenerates into covert exploitation. Domination is totally foreign to friendship because domination arises from, expresses, and reinforces inequality. Service between friends, in other words, realizes the pure ideal.[3]

Jesus' act of foot washing abolished inequality between him and his disciples. A slave could not be required to wash the feet of his master. It is a service one might freely render to a friend. Jesus laid aside his garments (13:4, 12) as he had spoken of laying down his life (10:18). The disciples were to have a "share" with him (v. 8); the washing of the feet expressed symbolically that they were brought into communion of life with Jesus through his death, a supreme act of self-giving and humble service. It is necessary to be washed by

Jesus, giver of life, if one is to have a part with him in eternal life—one must share in his death and resurrection.

Peter objected to the service roles between himself and Jesus (vv. 6–9). He had misunderstood the mysterious aspect of the deed implied in the question of Jesus: "Do you know what I have done to you?" (13:12). While he is indeed their Lord and Teacher, his loving service has transcended the inequality between them. "I have set you an example" (v. 15). The disciples are not to look only to his ultimate gesture of love; humble service should characterize all the living of his followers. Here is a moving lesson in *diakonia* (service). Jesus is indeed Lord and Teacher; he has authority. But his style and exercise of authority are marked by service. The whole of Jesus' life, culminating in his death and resurrection, was a passage from "this world" to the Father, from death to life, for us, "That...you may believe that I AM" (v. 19 ISV). He had spoken of his betrayal. He did not mean that betrayal as such would reveal Jesus as bearer of the divine name and power. He meant that the betrayal would trigger the procedure that would lead to his "lifting up" and his revelation of himself and the Father (see 8:28). The reality that Christ displays to us is himself as the "man for others." If we really receive him as such, we must ourselves become "people for others," servants of our fellows. Our challenge is our ongoing passage from selfishness to service (vv. 1–20).

Jesus had set an example (v. 14). He knew that his example would be ignored. Those who, down the ages, would claim to speak in his name would, too often, speak with arrogant self-assurance. He would, over and over, be betrayed.

Jesus' awareness of future betrayals was focused, here and now, on the presence of a traitor at his farewell supper. He declared, "One of you will betray me" (v. 21). A favorite disciple, not one of the Twelve, who reclined by him, asked who that person was. Jesus told him, quietly, that it was the one to whom he would hand a piece of bread he had dipped in the common dish. "When he had dipped the piece of bread, he gave it to Judas son of Simon Iscariot" (13:26).[4] That Jesus took bread occurs in all the gospel feeding stories and in the synoptic and Pauline Last Supper accounts. The phrase, to Christian ears, has unmistakable eucharistic overtones. Francis Moloney's comment is splendidly perceptive:

> Scribes could not tolerate the idea that the sharing of the morsel between Jesus and Judas might have eucharistic overtones and thus they eliminated words that made this association explicit. Just as baptism is a sub-theme to the footwashing, eucharist is a sub-theme to the meal and the gift of the morsel. Within the context of a meal indicated as eucharistic Jesus gave the morsel to the most despised character in the Johannine narrative: Judas. Disciples always have and always will display ignorance, fail Jesus, and deny him. Some may even betray him in an outrageous and public way. But Jesus' never-failing love for such disciples, a love that reached out even to the archetype of the evil disciple, reveals a unique God (see vv. 18–20). This is what it means to love *eis telos* (v. 1).[5]

Jesus had assured his own of how wholly he loved them. He would now speak to them his last will and testament. In verse 23, the Beloved Disciple puts in his first appearance. The betrayer, the one who "delivered him up" had gone to his task. For him "it was night" (v. 30)—he had turned his back on the light of the world. But he had not escaped the care of the shepherd (vv. 21–30).

After Judas's departure, Jesus was alone with his other disciples. In our text, the general context is that of Eucharist that, though never explicitly mentioned, is implied throughout. "Now the Son of Man has been glorified" (v. 31). The "now" is the hour of decision and consummation, belonging in time, yet decisive for eternity. Now, by going forward to the cross, by being "lifted up," Jesus is about to achieve his "glory"—his revelation of his loving Father. Already, he had told "the Jews," "Where I am going, you cannot come" (7:34; 8:21–22); but the reason on that occasion was their "sin." Here, the separation from his disciples is occasioned by his death. While they cannot come to him, he will come to them. In the meantime, they will live with his new "commandment." The "newness" here is the newness of the covenant founded and perpetuated in the Eucharist. What is new in this covenant is love "as I have loved you." Even if Jesus departs and they cannot now follow him to the Father, they can still be "followers" of Jesus here and now and they can keep his spirit alive among themselves (vv. 34–35). As long as they keep true to the "new commandment," as long as Christian love is in this world (the "Christian" love, too, of many who do not know him), the world still encounters Jesus.

DEPARTURE (CHAPTER 14)

Jesus spoke to console his friends, who were distressed over his words about going away. They ought not be troubled at a prospect of loneliness. He asks them to "believe" (14:1). Faith in Jesus is faith in God, accepting God for who he really is. His going from them is not abandonment; it is preparation of a home for them. There is ample room for them within the area of communion of life with himself and his Father. There is his Father's house and his own. Communion with Father and Son is his gift to them. He himself is the Way—a way that is the Truth and the Life. He is the Truth who makes known who God really is; he is the Life who makes known the one who is the source of life. Jesus himself is the Way to the ultimate destination, the final abiding with God. This road to God is a sure way because he is the one who leads us and takes us to our destination.

Jesus pointed beyond himself: "Whoever has seen me has seen the Father" (v. 9). He is the revelation of the Father. He is such because he is agent of the Father—the Sent One. He is in the Father and the Father in him because he bears the Father's name and authority. The believer in Son and Father does "the works" of the Father, manifests the union of Father and Son (see v. 12). In verses 1–11, Jesus had described his own closeness to God; in verses 12–14, he went on to indicate how others are brought into a like closeness.

This involves a journey: the journey of a believer (v. 12) inspired by hope (vv. 13–14) and love (vv. 15–17). Loving Jesus means listening to his word and putting it into action.

To obey is to love. Jesus "comes" to all who respond in this manner to his love. In response to his asking, the Father will give "another Paraclete." The term *parakletos*, meaning "assistant" or "advocate," occurs only in the Johannine writings. In 1 John 2:1, Jesus is a paraclete: "We have a *parakletos* with the Father, Jesus Christ the righteous." Jesus had been a paraclete to his disciples, helping them as their teacher, assisting them in their faith. Now, risen and with the Father (the post-Easter situation is really in view), he will be present to them in another manner.

The purpose of "the Spirit of truth" (the Paraclete), who is "in" and "with" the disciples, is to make Jesus present to them. That is why he can go on to promise: "I am coming to you" (v. 18). After the death and resurrection of Jesus, his Spirit is "with" the disciples, he dwells "among" them, he is "in" them. He is actively present in the awareness of the Johannine community. Through his Spirit–Paraclete presence, the message of Jesus had become an effective power in their lives.

Jesus did not leave his disciples orphaned and desolate. Indeed, by their faith, they would be able to "see" him and share in his life—in the life of Father and Son. Communion with him depends on their response to his word, for only by a loving response can they hope to be drawn into that communion of love. We learn that we cannot claim to be one with Jesus Christ, guided by and living according to his Spirit, unless we observe his demands in our everyday lives (vv. 15–24).

Jesus continued to speak encouragingly of his departure. Again, he referred to the Paraclete. The Father will send the Paraclete as he had sent Jesus, because the Paraclete is the continuation of Jesus' presence. Naturally, then, the Paraclete will continue to clarify Jesus' revelation. Jesus conferred the gift of peace, his shalom, the fullness of life. His return to the Father should not trouble the disciples. The declaration, "the Father is greater than I" (v. 28) balances the "Father and I are one" of chapter 10:30. Jesus reveals the Father and speaks in his name; that authority has been granted him. Jesus is about to clash, radically, with evil; before him, evil is ultimately helpless. As the Sent One, he always does as his Father commands. His "food" is to do the will of him who sent him (see 4:34). He will do what the Father wants: to make the Father truly known. The time has come to depart: "Let us be on our way" (v. 31). Clearly, an original ending! The logical continuation is chapter 18 (vv. 25–31). Here is a sign of the complex growth of the Fourth Gospel.

THE TRUE VINE (15:1—16:4A)

The image of the vine recalls the Old Testament designation of Israel as the vine of Yahweh (Isa 5:1–7; Jer 2:21; Ezek 15:1–8; Ps 80:8–19). Jesus declares that he himself, and not the Israel of old, is the real, the genuine, Vine of God. From this understanding of the image, we may move still further to stress the intimate relationship of branches and stock within the vine. And Jesus does stress the union between him and his disciples. As "true vine," Jesus is the source of real life. The Father remains the source of the productivity of the Vine.

The Vine (15:1–11)

"I am the vine, you are the branches" (v. 5). We tend to regard this statement as no more than a figure of speech. Spontaneously, for this is our way of thinking, we take the declaration about the vine to mean that the union of Christ with his own is like the link between the branches and the vine. The disciples are asked to think about a vine, to regard the vital link of branch and trunk. Jesus is thought to say, in effect: the union between us, between you and me, is something like that intimate union in nature. What he means is exactly the opposite! For him, that union of vine and branches is a symbol of the infinitely closer union of Jesus and his disciples. That is why Jesus can speak of himself as the *alethinos*, the "genuine" Vine: the sublime truth that the vine symbolizes is fully realized only in him. Understood in this manner, the declaration of Jesus is emphatic and clear: we live by the life of the Vine; we live by the life of Christ.

Christian life is unthinkable except in terms of Christ. There is, in verses 1–11, an emphasis on *menein*—"to abide": "Abide in me as I abide in you" (v. 4). Abiding is a mutual and shared relationship. Jesus and the Christian abide one in the other because they share a common life. The branches, however, while living from the sap of the vine, need to be tended. This is the task of the Father. He tends the vine, but its branches will bear fruit only if they are effectively attached to the vine, only if his life flows in them: apart from him, they can do nothing, they count for nothing. "Apart from me you can do nothing," as Jesus can do nothing without the Father (15:5). The Father expects the disciples, his children, to bear fruit. He is glorified—revealed—in the Son, in his obedience and in the perfect accomplishment of his work. It is a short, inevitable step to the glorification—the revelation—of the Father also in the obedience and fruitfulness of those who are joined to the Son. The Father's activity and that of the disciples come together in the production of fruit, with Jesus as the "vine" and the "place" where growth and fruit are achieved (vv. 1–8).

The intimate union of vine and branches, which the image had stressed, is now presented as a bond of love that unites the disciples of Christ (vv. 9–11). His affection for them is a friendship that knows no limits; he asks that all of them should love one another as friends and bear unmistakably the fruit of love. To abide in him, to love with his life, is to abide in his love, in the love with which he loves the disciples as the Father had loved him. Jesus had loved his own before he had chosen them; they are to abide in that love.

He went on to show what abiding in his love means. The love of Jesus was modeled on that of the Father. The fidelity of the disciples, in abiding in the divine life and under the divine care, should be modeled on the Son. As he has observed the commandments of his Father, so they should observe his. The parallel shows that love and obedience are mutually dependent: love arises out of obedience, obedience out of love. It follows that authentic Christian obedience can flourish only in an atmosphere of Christian love (vv. 9–11).

That is why the "command" to love is not as contradictory as it appears—one cannot "command" love!

Love One Another (15:12–17)

The "commandments" of Jesus may be reduced to one: the commandment of love. Love is the sap of the vine, the bond of existence within the unity of Father, Son, and believers. Jesus had hitherto granted to his disciples, to his own, obvious marks of affection and that from the moment he had chosen them (13:1). But now he is going to grant them the supreme evidence of his love. Voluntary death, a life freely laid down, will be the characteristic proof of *agape*, a love that moves out to sacrifice oneself for others. The statement that the greatest love is that which entails the supreme sacrifice is not, however, a definition of love; Jesus means that his sacrifice is the most expressive mark of it. The sense is that nobody can give a more convincing proof of love than one who offers one's life for those whom one loves. And when Jesus adds, "You are my friends," in effect, he is telling them that nobody has a greater love than that which he has for them. They had not chosen him. He had chosen and called them; he had chosen them to bear fruit. His first and last words: "love one another." They are not only his friends; they are friends one of the other.

Jesus had sketched for his disciples the program of the Christian apostolate: "You did not choose me but I chose you. And I appointed you to go out and bear fruit, fruit that will last" (v. 16). It is he who chooses, calls, and appoints; the initiative is entirely his. The principle of the apostolate is union with Jesus, but the disciples have a task to perform. By bearing the fruit that Jesus expects of them (fruit, even in the apostolate, which may well be hidden from eyes of flesh) they are true children of their heavenly Father. Then they can indeed address him as *Abba*; they can pray to him with absolute confidence.

As for Jesus, himself, he does not draft for his disciples an elaborate code of laws. He has no wish to impose a heavy burden on them. All that he commands them is reduced to one precept: "love one another." But he is not thereby less demanding. Substitution of the rule of law can effectively stifle further generosity. At any rate, there is no getting away from the fact that the one thing Jesus has asked of us—the one thing that Jesus has commanded us—is to love one another (vv. 12–17).

The World's Hatred (15:18—16:4a)

Jesus warned that down the road, disciples will be treated as he had been treated. They are not greater than their Master. They, as he, will be hated by the "world." Here, *kosmos* has, most emphatically, its hostile Johannine sense: the place of estrangement from God following on the rejection of both Jesus and the Father. The disciples do not belong to this "world"; they do not live by its standards. The "world" and discipleship are two clearly separated spheres. Jesus is going to the Father, but they will not be on their own at the mercy of that hostile "world." He will "send" the Paraclete as his "witness." The Paraclete will be the invisible but real presence of Jesus when he has gone to be with the Father. Tribulation will not be long in coming. "They will put you out of the synagogues" (16:2)—they will suffer the experience of the man born blind (see 9:22, 34). This reflects the experience of an early Jewish-Christian community. It is "their hour": reminiscent of Luke 22:53—"This is your hour, and the power of darkness!" The Evangelist is encouraging those of his day discouraged by opposition and persecution.

THE PARACLETE

In the farewell discourse, we have five passages in which the Paraclete appears, with the latest of them under the synonymous title "the Spirit of Truth": 14:16–17; 14:25–26; 15:26–27; 16:7–11; 16:13–15. The Paraclete is the divine power that continues and completes Jesus' ministry. The Paraclete is the perpetuation of Jesus' presence among his followers, the presence of Jesus after Jesus had departed. This emerges clearly in chapter 16, "I tell you the truth: it is to your advantage that I go away, for if I do not go away, the Advocate will not come to you; but if I go, I will send him to you" (v. 7). The departure of Jesus is a paradox. He had assured his disciples, "I will not leave you orphaned" (14:18). Yet, they must suffer the loss of him as Jesus if they are to have his abiding presence as Paraclete, for the Spirit is a gift of the glorified Lord and remains essentially related to Jesus. This point was made in 7:39: "As yet there was no Spirit, because Jesus was not yet glorified." The risen Jesus gives the Spirit because it is as Paraclete he will henceforth be present on earth. The statement about Jesus' departure (16:7) becomes, paradoxically, a promise of his presence, albeit in a different manner. Jesus had already said that the Paraclete would testify on his behalf (15:26). He had warned that the "world" that had hated him would hate his followers (15:18–20). Now we learn that the witness-bearing Paraclete reveals the conflict state of the Church.

"When he comes, he will prove the world wrong about sin and righteousness and judgment: about sin, because they do not believe in me; about righteousness, because I am going to the Father and you will see me no longer; about judgment, because the ruler of this world has been condemned" (16:8–11). This is nothing other than an anticipation of, and a reversal of, the trial of Jesus. The Paraclete is witness and revealer of the truth; he will show the disciples "where wrong and right and judgment lie" (16:8 NEB). He will prove the world guilty of sin—the basic (Johannine) sin of rejecting the light, of refusing to accept Jesus. He will prove the world wrong about righteousness by showing that Jesus, whom it branded guilty, is the righteous One. He will demonstrate, with typical Johannine irony, that in condemning Jesus, the world brought judgment on itself. The cross seemed to be the end, the triumph of the world. In the Paraclete, Jesus is still present and the tables have been turned: "And I, when I am lifted up from the earth, will draw all people to myself" (12:32). The hour of passion and death was the moment of naked confrontation of Jesus and evil (12:31; 14:30). Victory over death, the Father's vindication of Jesus, meant that the power of evil had been broken. The Paraclete will not only spell out for the disciples the measure of these events, but his abiding presence with them will be the comforting assurance of the victory of their Lord: "Take courage; I have conquered the world!" (16:33).

In John 14:25–26, the Paraclete, who takes Jesus' place, will teach, leading into a fuller understanding of what Jesus had revealed and taught. In 13:13–15, this role of the Paraclete as teacher surfaces again. "When the Spirit of truth comes, he will guide you into all the truth; for he will not speak on his own, but will speak whatever he hears, and he will declare to you the things that are to come. He will glorify me, because he will take what is mine and declare it to you" (16:13–14). The language is opaque, as not infrequently in John. It is so here because Jesus is speaking obliquely of his future presence. Jesus had told the disciples: "I still have many things to say to you, but you cannot bear them now" (16:12). Only after his "glorification"—his full revelation of the Father and of himself—could there be understanding of what was said and done throughout his ministry. After the resurrection, the Paraclete will guide them into the full meaning of Jesus and of his teaching. If he leads them into all the truth, he still will not speak on his own. There is no new revelation because there cannot be new revelation: Jesus is the revelation of the Father, the Word. But what does it mean that the Paraclete will reveal the things that are to come? Rather than an announcement of a new revelation, this means a spelling out to successive generations the significance of what Jesus had said and done.

In the Fourth Gospel, the Spirit—under the title *Paraclete*—is the perpetuation of Jesus' presence. The

Johannine community was convinced that their Lord abode with them. His continuing presence among his own would no longer be in the figure of the man of Galilee but as life-giving Spirit. As Jesus had been "Teacher and Lord" of his disciples (13:13), so now as Paraclete, he was the sole authority of the community. In the Johannine writings, there is, strikingly, no evidence of any "ecclesiastical" structure. The Paraclete is the ultimate authority. This, surely, is why the Paraclete is so prominent in these chapters. One must acknowledge that it is extremely difficult to pin down a precise understanding of Paraclete/Spirit. It is clear, however, that the Spirit is experienced as the Johannine community's Teacher and Interpreter. "It is possible to say that the only person who will understand the words about the Spirit is one who has already experienced the presence of the Spirit."[6]

The discourse ends (16:16–33) with words of assurance to the disciples. They had progressed in their understanding of him, but they had not yet grasped the significance of his departure. The "hour" is, paradoxically, the moment of revelation of the Father (v. 25) and the moment of flight and abandonment (v. 32). In the midst of tribulation, they are to be bolstered by the prospect of future joy (vv. 20–22; see 14:1, 27). They are disciples of a Jesus who is victorious in the darkest moment of abandonment and death (v. 23). "I am not alone because the Father is with me" (v. 32). As in Mark 14:50, the disciples may be scattered (John 16:32) and Jesus left alone. But never would the Johannine Jesus cry out, "My God, my God, why have you forsaken me?" (Mark 15:34; see John 12:27–28). The closing word of Jesus is a resounding word of encouragement: "In the world you face persecution. But take courage; I have conquered the world!" (John 16:33). A Johannine disciple had heard this word: "This is the victory that conquers the world, our faith. Who is it that conquers the world but the one who believes that Jesus is the Son of God?" (1 John 5:4–5).

JESUS' CLOSING PRAYER (CHAPTER 17)

The Farewell Discourse closes with a prayer. This prayer is, in its manner, a commentary on the passion of Jesus that reflects the drift of the Fourth Gospel's emphasis: the coming of Jesus, revealer of the Father, into this world (17:1–12), then the return of Jesus to the Father. Structurally, the prayer falls into three parts as Jesus prays for himself (vv. 1–5), for his disciples (vv. 6–29), and for the community of the future, those who "believe . . . through their word" (vv. 20–26).

For Himself (17:1–5)

"The hour has come," the hour of death and resurrection. It is the hour of the glory of Jesus, "glory" being the revelation of God in power. Only in death and resurrection does Jesus fully reveal himself and reveal the Father. And only by laying down his life for his friends, out of love, is Jesus able to give the life-giving Spirit (7:39). "Glorify your Son": the "glorifying" of the Son necessarily involves the glorifying of the Father—making the Father known because the self-disclosure of Jesus is geared to the revelation of the unseen God.

If the Son has been given power over "all flesh"—all humankind—it is that he may bestow "eternal life." Eternal life is "knowledge": to leave oneself free to receive eternal life, one must "know," one must have experienced the loving relationship of Father and Son. Here, "to know," as in the Old Testament, means to have communion with God. A revealing parallel is found in 1 John 1:3—"our fellowship is with the Father and with his Son Jesus Christ" where "fellowship" (*koinonia*) is the same as "to know" in our text. Jesus' whole concern had been to make the Father known. Yet, the "hour" of his death and resurrection is the high moment of that revelation. So Jesus prays to the Father.

For His Disciples (17:6–19)

In verses 6–19, Jesus prays for his disciples. He prays for those present at the meal (chap. 13)—he had taken care to make the Father known to them. Indeed, they were the Father's gift to him in the first place. They know that the Father is the source of all that Jesus had done for them. Jesus had given them "the words" of the Father—he had revealed the Father. Jesus had come into the world because God so loved the world that he gave his only Son (3:16) in order to save the world of humankind (3:17). Jesus, who is now sending his disciples into the world to speak again his word of salvation, cannot pray for that hostile world. The disciples are being sent, as Jesus was sent, to challenge the world, so that people might at last turn from darkness to light. He prays for those whom he leaves behind to carry on his work. He commits them to the Father's care and prays especially that they may experience among themselves the warm communion of Father and Son.

Though regularly unperceived, verse 12 raises a basic issue: the question of divine mercy and forgiveness. "I guarded them, and not one of them was lost except the one destined to be lost" (17:12). This rendering reflects the current verdict, traditionally and of scholars, that Judas is envisaged. It is essential to decide how one understands the expression: *ho huios tes apoleias.* Translated as "the one destined to be lost" it is, literally, "the son of perdition" (NRSV margin, "the son of destruction"). The expression occurs again only in 2 Thessalonians 2:3, 8–9, where it refers to a Satanic figure. John, then, is referring to Satan, not Judas.

Often regarded as a reference to Judas, this expression must be given the meaning it has in the only other place it appears in the New Testament: Satan (2 Thess 2:3, 8–9). The only person in the story Jesus could not "care for" is Satan who planned the betrayal (cf. 13:2). Jesus washed the feet and shared the morsel with Judas despite Satan's designs (cf. 13:2). Jesus has kept and cared for all the disciples entrusted to him by the Father, including Judas. As his gestures in 13:1–17, 21–38 indicate, not even Judas can be judged as lost.[7]

One makes an issue of this because of a concern with a perennial human penchant to trivialize the wondrous mercy and forgiveness of God. Jesus was well aware of this (see Luke 15:1–32; Matt 18:23–35). This attitude finds unsavory expression in the demonization of Judas. In John 12:6, he had become a petty thief. It was assumed that he had to have come to a sticky end—hence two, wholly contradictory, versions of his death: Matthew 27:3–10 and Acts 1:18–20. We should learn that we are better advised to leave not only others, but ourselves as well in the hands of a merciful, forgiving, and infinitely loving God—the God whose love reached the limit: he did not spare his own Son.[8]

Verse 13 opens the theme of Jesus' return to his Father. He speaks, while he is still with them, so that the disciples he is leaving behind may find the joy that follows on the fulfillment of the commandment of love. In bearing witness before the world, they must, as he, suffer the world's hate. But that is a feature of their task as it was of his. The Father will "protect them from the evil one" (v. 15)—surely an echo of the Lord's Prayer (Matt 6:13). The disciples will be consecrated in the truth—in God's Word; the truth that is Jesus' revelation of the unseen God. To be consecrated in the truth means to have a closer union with Jesus who is Truth (14:6). They have accepted him and kept his word (17:6–14); now they must bring him and his words to others. Jesus sends them as he himself was sent; the mission of his community of faith is to continue the mission of Jesus. By his death—his "sanctification"—Jesus will confirm and consecrate his disciples. His death is a sacrifice: the supreme priestly action on their behalf.

For the Community (17:20–26)

The mission of the disciples (vv. 6–19) will be efficacious, made so by the prayer of Jesus. The power of his prayer reaches out to those others, those who will come to "believe in him"; for faith means a personal relationship with Jesus, union with him. And Jesus prays that the community be one.

Unity follows on the communion of Christians with Father and Son. The missionary role is not lost to sight: "that the world may believe." Those later disciples, like the initial group, are sent, as the Master was, "to testify to the truth" (18:37). "Glory" will be theirs as, in their turn and manner, they make Father and Son known. But they can have this "glory," this revealing role, only if they are one with Father and Son and with one another. Only so will they be witnesses to a God who is love.

As Jesus had come into the world to do the saving will of the Father and, the task accomplished (19:30), to return in glory to that beloved Father, so he wills and prays that his disciples, when they have accomplished their task, will enjoy unending blessedness with him. Then, for them too, the message that they had preached will be wholly clear. They will see, and share in, the perfect union of Father and Son and glow in their love. All will be achieved in and through their being with Jesus, fully and forever. It is because the Father had given them to the Son, and because they had been joined with him on earth, as branches of the Vine, that they will be united with him forever. They are those who have known Father and Son, and that is the eternal life (17:3).

The closing words of the prayer bring us back to earth. Jesus will make the Father more deeply known. But that will be at the cost of love. It is only as a loving community that the love of Father and Son can be experienced. Jesus prays not only that the love of the Father for the Son will be in them, but that he himself will be in them—"and I in them" (v. 26). This refers to Jesus abiding (as the glorified Christ) with his community. He is the constant presence of God in the community. But it is in loving one another that the disciples can be one with Jesus. Only so will he really dwell among them and be in them. It is the earnest prayer of Jesus that this be so: "I ask not only on behalf of these, but also on behalf of those who will believe in me through their word, that they may all be one" (17:20–21).

As the hour approached, Jesus was set on assuring his disciples how utterly he loved them. His washing of their feet was a moving gesture. It was also a challenge to them. He was faithful to all of his own.

He spoke at length to console his friends, saddened at his speaking of departure. He will not leave them orphaned: he will come to them, as the Paraclete, to abide with them. They must remember that they are branches of him, the Vine—branches that should bear fruit—and realize that without him they are helpless. They are not his servants; they are his friends. They will be deprived of him for a little while. He will see them again and they will rejoice. And they will have the assurance that he had conquered the world.

In his closing solemn prayer, Jesus prayed for himself, for the consolation of his disciples, and for all down the ages who, fruit-bearing branches of the Vine, would continue his task.

Notes

1. Charles Dickens, *A Tale of Two Cities* (London: Ballantyne, Hanson & Co., 1902), 454.

2. Sandra M. Schneiders, *Written That You May Believe: Encountering Jesus in the Fourth Gospel* (New York: Crossroad, 1999), 169–74.

3. Schneiders, *Written That You May Believe*, 171f.

4. Thereby hangs a tale. Some early manuscripts of the Gospel omit "he took it"—it is not in the NRSV, the version followed here; it ought to be!

5. Francis J. Moloney, *The Gospel of John* (Collegeville, MN: Liturgical Press, 1998), 384.

6. Rudolph Schnackenburg, *The Gospel According to St. John*, vol. 3 (New York: Crossroad, 1982), 153.

7. Moloney, *The Gospel of John*, 467f.

8. Wilfrid Harrington, *From the Presence of the Lord: A God Too Gracious* (Dublin: Columba Press, 2006), 55–64.

CHAPTER 6

DEATH AND LIFE

When Jesus had ended the solemn prayer (chap. 17), he went with his disciples across the Kidron valley to a garden. Judas, who knew the place, guided a Roman military attachment and some temple police. Jesus, fully aware of all that was to happen, took the initiative and strode forward to accost the band. They declared that they sought "Jesus of Nazareth." At the God-presence in him, manifest in his affirmation "I am" (*ego eimi*), they were rendered powerless, stricken to the ground. Jesus, wholly in charge of the situation, laid down his terms: they may arrest him on condition that they did not detain his disciples. Judas is included among those who must be permitted to go free. "I did not lose a single one of those whom you gave me" (18:9): a paraphrase of the assurances of 6:39 and 17:12. Judas, too, had been given by the Father, and he stands within the Father's loving care. Simon Peter struck out impetuously and cut off the right ear of Malchus; he was rebuked by Jesus. Only now was Jesus arrested, and only because he permitted it.

THE PASSION (18:12—19:42)

John presents the passion as the triumph of the Son of God. The *dramatis personae* are sharply characterized. Despite appearances, Jesus is always in control. He is the Judge who judges his judge (Pilate) and his accusers ("the Jews"). He is the King who reigns, with the cross for a throne: "I, when I am lifted up from the earth, will draw all people to myself" (12:32). "The Jews" are not the whole Jewish people but its leaders who see Jesus as a danger to them, the establishment, and who are determined to destroy him.

Such are "the Jews" in the storyline. For John and his contemporaries, "the Jews" are the leaders of a later Judaism vigorously opposed to the now distinctive Christian movement. Pilate recognizes—and three times acknowledges—the innocence of Jesus. He desperately tries to compromise but gives up by yielding to political blackmail. He is a man who strives to avoid making a decision for or against Jesus—and finds himself trapped.

Jesus Before Pilate (18:28—19:16a)

The synoptic accounts of the trial before Pilate tell us little, whereas John's dramatic reconstruction does bring out the significance of it. Only John makes clear why Jesus was brought to Pilate in the first place and why Pilate gave in to having him crucified. Only John shows the interplay of subtle (and not so subtle) political forces on Pilate and indicates how Pilate's original questioning of Jesus concerned a political charge against him. Yet Mark, we now realize, has given the key to the trial in the title "King of the Jews" (15:2). Thereafter, he stresses that it is as King of the Jews (Messiah) that Jesus is rejected by the crowd and crucified. In John, this theme of Jesus' royal status dominates the encounter between Pilate and Jesus (John 18:33, 37, 39; 19:3, 13, 14, 15, 19–20). Recognition or rejection of it is the decisive issue for Pilate and "the Jews." It is they who are on trial.

There is a further theological reason for John's stress on the Roman trial. We are to view Pilate in the light of the rest of the Fourth Gospel. He provides an example of an attitude to Jesus that purports to be neither faith nor rejection: the typical attitude of those who try to maintain a middle position in an all-or-nothing situation. Pilate's reluctance to make a decision for or against the Light leads to disaster. Because Pilate will not face the challenge of deciding for the Truth in Jesus and against "the Jews," he thinks he can persuade "the Jews" to accept a solution that will make it unnecessary for him to declare for Jesus. This is the Johannine view of the episodes of Barabbas, the scourging, and the delivery of Jesus to the Jews as "your King." For John, the trial is our own tragic history of temporizing and indecision. Pilate, the would-be neutral man, is frustrated by the pressure of others. He failed to listen to the truth and declare in its favor. He and all who would follow him inevitably end up enslaved to this world.

The Johannine presentation of the Roman trial is highly dramatic.[1] It is structured in seven episodes or scenes. There are two settings or stages: the outside court of the praetorium where "the Jews" are gathered; the inside room where Jesus is held prisoner. Pilate moves back and forth from one stage to the other. The atmosphere is notably different in either setting. Inside, Jesus and Pilate engage in calm dialogue; outside is clamorous as Pilate is pressured to find Jesus guilty. Pilate's passing from one setting to the other is expressive of an internal struggle: while becoming increasingly convinced of Jesus' innocence, he finds himself being forced to condemn him.

Scene 1: Outside — "The Jews" Demand Death (18:28b–32)

"The Jews" who had brought Jesus to Pilate would not enter the Gentile praetorium. To do so would involve ritual defilement and prevent them from celebrating Passover. Pilate went out to them; they insisted that Jesus was a criminal deserving death. The execution would be according to Roman law: death by crucifixion (12:33). Jesus had already referred to his death as a "lifting up"—on a cross! "And I, when I am lifted up from the earth, will draw all people to myself" (12:32).

Scene 2: Inside — Jesus and Pilate on Kingship (18:33–38a)

Pilate questioned Jesus: "Are you the King of the Jews?" (18:33). Jesus wanted to know how he understood the title: in a political or in a religious sense? He himself proclaimed the otherworldly realm of truth; he separated his kingdom from anything that could threaten Pilate. His purpose was to bear witness to "the way things really are"—the way God is, the way God is related to the world. "What is truth?" (v. 38)—Pilate rejected Jesus' offer. His way is not the way of God.

Scene 3: Outside — Pilate Finds Jesus Not Guilty (18:38b–40)

Pilate had shown that he was not on the side of truth. He had turned from the light. He was the one on trial. He went outside and declared that, having interrogated Jesus, he could find no case against him. Verse 38a is the first of Pilate's "not guilty" statements (see 19:4, 6). He tried the ploy of the Passover amnesty: "Do you want me to release for you the King of the Jews?" (v. 39). They shouted back, "Not this man, but Barabbas!" (v. 40)—a notorious bandit.

Scene 4: Inside — Soldiers Scourge Jesus (19:1–3)

Pilate, in failing to grant Jesus justice, is forced to a travesty of justice. He ordered Jesus to be scourged. Scourged, even though he had already pronounced him innocent! His scourging of an innocent man proves that man's innocence! (v. 4). Pilate is getting more deeply embroiled. The soldiers twisted some thorn branches into a mock crown (diadem) and decked Jesus in a cast-off soldier's cloak. They saluted him: "Hail, King of the Jews!" (v. 3). The kingship theme, already introduced in the dialogue with Pilate, would persist. Ironically, this mockery serves as a declaration of who Jesus is. John strengthens the kingship motif. In the Synoptic narrative, Jesus was stripped of his "regal" trappings (see Mark 15:20). In John, Jesus goes to the cross dressed as a king.

Scene 5: Outside — "Here Is the Man!" (19:4–8)

Pilate had Jesus presented to the crowd—all bloody as he was from the scourging and decked in the mock crown and robes. "Here is the man!"(v. 5). Showing them a pathetic human being who was no threat to either Rome or "the Jews," Pilate declared, "I am bringing him out to you" (v. 4). But Jesus "came out" (v. 5): he is still master of his destiny. The episode is an ironical presentation of Jesus as Son of Man. The crowd howled for his death: "Crucify him!" In exasperation, Pilate retorted, "Take him yourselves and crucify him; I find no case against him" (v. 6). They shot back, "According to [our] law he ought to die because he has claimed to be the Son of God" (v. 7). Here is the theological reason why "the Jews" had brought Jesus to trial before Pilate. At the time of the Fourth Gospel, this claim was emerging as the great issue between Jews and Christians—viewed by the former as a threat to monotheism.

Scene 6: Inside — Pilate and Jesus on Power (19:9–11)

Pilate was now quite alarmed: the unbelieving politician is superstitious. He came inside and asked Jesus, "Where are you from?" (v. 9)—the fundamental question of Johannine Christology. Jesus was silent. When Pilate invoked his authority he was told bluntly, "You would have no power over me unless it had been given you from above; therefore the one who handed me over to you is guilty of a greater sin" (v. 11). Jesus is "from above" and his authority is from above. Pilate was now desperately anxious to release Jesus. He had been challenged by Truth—and had sought to compromise. He was hopelessly trapped. His next attempt to have the case dismissed was met with naked blackmail: "If you release this man, you are no friend of the emperor. Everyone who claims to be a king sets himself against the emperor" (v. 12). Pilate was aware that his standing in Rome was, just then, not very secure; he could not risk a suggestion of disloyalty to the emperor. Time had run out on him. He could no longer evade a decision.

Scene 7: Outside — "The Jews" Obtain the Death Sentence (19:12–16a)

Pilate yielded to the Jewish demand for Jesus' crucifixion. John's account of the passing of the sentence of death is detailed, dramatic, and theological. The only points of parallel with the Synoptics are in the repeated call for crucifixion and the outcome of Jesus being "handed over." The background to this verb (*paradidomi*), used by all the evangelists, implied that Jesus was "delivered up" to his enemies "according to the definite plan and foreknowledge of God" (Acts 2:23); there was a mysterious divine purpose. The real trial was over, when "the Jews" uttered the fateful words "We have no king but the emperor" (John 19:15). This is akin to the statement in Matthew's account: "His blood be on us and on our children!" (Matt 27:25). Both evangelists are reflecting not history but apologetic theology. The tragedy of Jesus' death was viewed through the hostility between church and synagogue in the late first century CE. The audience at the trial is made to voice a Christian interpretation of the Jewish rejection of Jesus.

John also tells us that this was the hour when the Passover lambs were being sacrificed in the temple. It is supreme Johannine irony: "the Jews" renounce the covenant at the very moment when the priests begin to prepare for the feast that annually recalled God's deliverance of his covenanted people. By the blood of a lamb in Egypt, Yahweh had marked them off to be spared as his own. Now they know no king but the emperor and they slay another lamb. At that moment, just before the Passover, as Jesus set out for Golgotha to shed his saving blood, the trial of Jesus ends with the fulfillment of that proclamation at the start of the Gospel: "Here is the Lamb of God who takes away the sin of the world!" (1:29).

The Crucifixion of Jesus (19:16b–27)

Jesus was led out, laden with the crossbeam and without human assistance, to Golgotha, the Place of the Skull. "Carrying the cross by himself" (v. 17)—there is no Simon of Cyrene: John's Christology has no room for Jesus' needing or accepting help. Jesus was crucified between two others. Pilate had ordered an inscription that was affixed to the cross: "Jesus of Nazareth, the King of the Jews." He had the notice written in Hebrew, Latin, and Greek. The annoyed "Jews" protested: "Do not write, 'The King of the Jews,' but, 'This man said, I am King of the Jews.'" Pilate retorted, "What I have written I have written" (vv. 21–22). As representative of imperial Rome, Pilate had made a heraldic proclamation, couched in the sacred and secular languages of the day—a worldwide proclamation of Jesus' kingship. Supreme irony! This King is drawing all people to himself (see 12:32).

In John 19:25–27, John has, by the cross, the Mother of Jesus and the Beloved Disciple. The Mother of Jesus was the first person in the story to trust unconditionally in the word of Jesus (2:3–5). Now, lifted up on the cross, Jesus bids her accept the Beloved Disciple as her son. He bids that model disciple accept the Mother of Jesus as his mother. Jesus had established a new family. "Because of the cross and from the moment of the cross a new family of Jesus has been created. The Mother of Jesus, a model of faith, and the disciple whom Jesus loved and held close to himself are one as the disciple accepts the Mother in an unconditioned acceptance of the word of Jesus."[2]

The scene is surely symbolic as a new relationship is set up between the mother and the disciple. The disciple "took her into his own home" (19:27). The model disciple obeys unquestioningly the word of Jesus. Mark tells us that, at the crucifixion, "there were also women looking on from a distance" (Mark 15:40; see Matt 27:55; Luke 23:49) and makes no mention of the mother or of any male disciple. It is wholly unlikely that women and a follower of the condemned Jesus would have been permitted to stand at the very place of execution. Here the theological creativity of John is very much in evidence.

Jesus' Last Words (19:28–30)

Jesus was conscious that his hour had drawn to its close; all had now been accomplished. In response to his call, "I am thirsty," John notes that a sponge soaked in sour wine was raised to his lips "on a branch of hyssop"—a small plant that could not sustain a sponge (vv. 28–29). Pointedly, in Exodus 12:22, it is specified that hyssop be used to sprinkle the blood of the Passover lamb on the doorposts of the Israelite homes. Plausibly, John introduced the unlikely hyssop here to suggest that Jesus was fulfilling the role of the Passover lamb. The last word of Jesus, "It is finished" is a cry of victory: now Jesus will draw all people to himself. "Then he bowed his head and gave up his spirit" (v. 30). The bowing of the head was a deliberate gesture. "The image is of Jesus looking down on the assembled group and, now that the hour of his glorification has come, he gives the Spirit to his followers."[3] In John 7:37–39, Jesus promised that when he was glorified, those who believed in him would receive the Spirit. His last breath was the outpouring of the life-giving Spirit—his Spirit.

Aftermath of the Death (19:31–37)

The final details, the not breaking of Jesus' legs and the flow of blood and water, have no parallel in the Synoptics. True Passover Lamb, not one bone of Jesus was broken (see Exod 12:46). The flow of blood and water is another proleptic reference to the giving of the Spirit, following on John 19:30. There is more to it. Remarkable is verse 35, the narrator's insistent testimony to that flow of blood and water. It is surely a word to the reader. The "water" of baptism (see 3:5) and the "blood" of the Eucharist (see 6:34, 54, 55–56) are here linked with the cross. Jesus, physically absent from the community, is, nonetheless, present in Spirit (19:30), baptism, and Eucharist. The Johannine community is urged "to believe" this, to take it to heart. Notice that blood and water flow from the dead Jesus. The drama of the cross does not end in death but in the flow of life that comes from death. The death of Jesus on the cross is the beginning of Christian life.

The Burial of Jesus (19:38–42)

Joseph of Arimathea, a recent disciple of Jesus, got permission from Pilate to remove the body of Jesus. He and that other secret disciple, Nicodemus, now "came out" and gave Jesus a royal burial. They bound his body in linen cloths, sprinkling a lavish quantity of perfumed spices between the folds. Then they laid him in a new unused tomb in a nearby garden. The whole is historically quite at odds with the "dishonorable burial" account in Mark 15:42–47. It is wholly in keeping with the Johannine presentation of the kingly stature of Jesus. Interestingly, the passion story had opened in a garden (18:1) and ends in a garden (19:41).

THE RESURRECTION (20:1–29)

John has preserved two versions of what, in the Synoptic tradition, is the women's visit to the tomb, John 20:1–3 and 11–13. Underlying the first of them (vv. 1–2) would seem to be the earliest form of an empty tomb narrative in any gospel. John has introduced the Beloved Disciple and has, for his own dramatic purpose, reduced the original group of women to Mary Magdalene, preparing the way for the later

Christophany to her (vv. 14–18). It is this Christophany, and not an angelic spokesman, that explains the meaning of the empty tomb (vv. 12–13). But the tradition that was thus rewritten is very early indeed. In verses 1–2, Mary Magdalene is not a believer but a woman quite confused.

Thoroughly Johannine is 20:1–10. At Mary's disturbing news (v. 2), "Peter and the other disciple" hurried to the tomb. In the tradition, Peter's companion was unnamed. John has introduced him as the Beloved Disciple so that his coming to faith might interpret the significance of the empty tomb. The burial cloths and, more unexpectedly, their arrangement, are a sign that Mary's understanding of the empty tomb ("They have taken the Lord out of the tomb" 20:2) is not the correct one. Jesus had not been "taken" anywhere. Rather, he had left mortality behind him. Only the Beloved Disciple (vv. 2, 8) seeing the sign, believed—"He saw and believed" (v. 8). Manifestly, he believed, even before any appearance of the risen Lord, in the risen Christ, himself. The fact of the matter is that while the "Beloved Disciple" is a real person and the source of John's tradition, he also represents the Christian disciple who is sensitive, in faith and love, to the presence of the risen Jesus. With this one theological exception of the Beloved Disciple, who saw with eyes of faith, the "empty tomb" is never regarded as a reason for faith. The conviction that the body of Jesus can no longer be found in the tomb because he is risen (and not for any other reason) follows on encounter with the risen Lord.

What is the significance of the resurrection of Jesus? The confession, "God raised Jesus from the dead," implies more, much more, than the deed of raising from death. It implies that the kingdom of God—the rule of God—has indeed come in Jesus. The resurrection should not be regarded in isolation. In declaring, "Christ is risen," one is acknowledging that God's saving purposes have been accomplished in Jesus. Jesus had viewed his whole life and his whole mission in relation to the fulfillment of such promises. It was because of their former hope in him that the disciples were able to interpret the resurrection as God's confirmation of all that Jesus stood for. Because he was raised from the dead, Jesus holds decisive significance for us. Because of the fact of his resurrection, we know that meaningless death—and meaningless life—now have meaning. Jesus died with the cry on his lips: "My God, my God, why have you forsaken me?" (Mark 15:34). The sequel was to show that God had never abandoned Jesus. We have the assurance that he will not abandon us. We do, for our comfort, need Markan Christology to balance the Johannine.

Jesus Appears to Mary Magdalene (20:11–18)

Mary, at the tomb (vv. 11–13) has not advanced beyond the confusion of verses 1–2. Quite like Luke's Emmaus story where the two disciples conversed with "the stranger" (Luke 24:13–19), Mary speaks with this "stranger" (John 20:14–15). She recognized him at his calling her by name. This reminds us of John 10:3—the Good Shepherd, who "calls his own sheep by name." Her joyous instinct was to cling to him. She has to learn that the time of association with the earthly Jesus is past. His "hour" is still in process—the "hour" of death, resurrection, and return to the Father. Mary is given a mission: being an apostle to the disciples. She brings an astounding message. Up to now, in the narrative, Jesus alone was Son. Now, he speaks of my Father and your Father, my God and your God! The God and Father of Jesus is God and Father of his "brothers." Christians are no longer Jesus' disciples, not even his "friends" (15:15) but his brothers and sisters. Mary Magdalene went—a journey that was a journey of faith. "I have seen the Lord" (20:18); she also had reached the fullness of Johannine faith. "Another foundational character from the earliest Christian community has journeyed from the darkness of unfaith through a partial faith into perfect belief."[4]

In the House (20:19–29)

Although the disciples had been assured by Mary Magdalene that the Lord was risen, they hide away "for fear of the Jews" (v. 19); the message of the good news does not spare Christians from fear. Jesus came to dispel their fear and bring the peace that only he can grant. At his death, Jesus had breathed his Spirit on that little family at the foot of the cross. Now he breathes the Spirit upon this community.

It is significant that, in John's Gospel, the church is founded by the risen Lord. When Jesus breathed upon the disciples, a new creation was taking place. Just as God made "the man" into a living being by breathing life into him (Gen 2:7) and, as in Ezekiel 37, the dead bones of Israel were stirred to life by the breath of God, so the life of the Church came from the breath of the Spirit of Jesus. This is the new, eternal life brought into being by Jesus, and it plays such a major role in John's Gospel. In this sense, everything is already accomplished when Jesus breathes life into his disciples. And he entrusts them with a mission. The mission is nothing more or less than the one he had received from the Father and, indeed, accomplished by his death and resurrection: the reconciliation of men and women with their Parent (the forgiveness of sin). To carry out their mission, they are enlivened and inspired by the Holy Spirit, which is Christ's Spirit, making them one with him. They are to be Christ to the world. They will be channels of God's forgiveness of sin and will lay bare sinfulness.

The episode of Thomas (vv. 24–29) is of great importance for the Fourth Evangelist and is, indeed, climactic in his Gospel. The disciple, Thomas, passed from unbelief to belief. Thomas had refused to accept the word of the other disciples and insisted on having personal proof of the reality of the resurrection of Jesus (vv. 24–25). In the event, he came to belief without need of the crude verification he had seemed to demand (20:25, 27–28). It was enough to have seen (v. 29). Nonetheless, verse 27 is the assurance that the risen Jesus is the crucified Jesus. It is unfortunate that Thomas has been remembered for his stubbornness—"doubting Thomas." He deserves to be remembered for the most forthright confession of faith in the Gospel: "My Lord and my God" (v. 28). The text should be interpreted in the same manner as similar texts in chapter 12—"Whoever sees me sees the Father" and "the Father and I are one." As the Sent One, Jesus is, at a deep level, one with the Father. Today we might say that Jesus is wholly transparent to God. Thomas's confession is an acknowledgment and proclamation of the God revealed in Jesus. It is, likely, a confessional formula of the Evangelist's Church.

Thomas has made the last utterance of a disciple of Jesus. The Evangelist adds a comment that is crucial for all disciples of the risen Lord. "Have you believed because you have seen me? Blessed are those who have not seen and yet have come to believe" (v. 29). The Evangelist is writing for a generation that has not "seen" the Lord, for whom Jesus is absent. Here is a word of consolation. This later generation of believers is not less privileged than the foundational disciples. They share with them a common faith in the Lord, though he be not visible. In a sense, they are more blessed; they have believed without seeing. We recall that the Beloved Disciple had already believed without seeing (20:8). These Johannine Christians are his true disciples as are we of subsequent generations.

THE CONCLUSION OF THE GOSPEL (20:30–31)

Christians who have not seen and yet believed have been declared blessed. Now, in this conclusion, they are told that all that has gone before, in this Gospel, has been written for them. In the story, disciples, again and again, were summoned from unfaith, through partial faith, into authentic faith. The readers are presumed to have attained genuine faith. They are now being urged to persist in their faith and to deepen it:

"But these are written so that you may come to believe" (v. 31). They are to believe, wholly, that Jesus is Messiah, a Messiah who is Son of God. He is the "one sent" who has made the Father fully known. As such, he is giver of eternal life. They have this life in virtue of their believing relationship with him.

It is the desire of the author of the Gospel that all those who read this book or hear its proclamation be a community of beloved disciples. The book was written so that a narrative that reports how Jesus had lived his story might confirm what was proclaimed in the Prologue. The author believes passionately that Jesus' life story proves the claims made for him in the Prologue.[5]

The conclusion to the Fourth Gospel, which states its purpose, also states the purpose of all four Gospels. All of them are concerned with Christology and discipleship. They are written to deepen understanding of Jesus so that deeper knowledge of him and faith in him will inspire and lead to a richer life of discipleship.

EPILOGUE (21:21–25)

The Gospel proper has ended at 20:30–31. Chapter 21 is an appendix. After an introductory listing of the disciples concerned (vv. 1–3), we have an appearance of Jesus by the lakeside, a miraculous catch of fish, Peter's reaction, followed by breakfast with Jesus (vv. 4–14). Finally, there is the commissioning of Peter and a prophecy of his death (vv. 15–19). The chapter is built around Peter and the Beloved Disciple. In a fishing scene and at a meal, Jesus reveals himself to his disciples; he invites them to faith. The ease and intimacy of his meeting with them is reminiscent of their first meeting (1:37–39). Yet, the disciples had difficulty in recognizing him (vv. 4, 12). This is a constant feature of the resurrection narratives in all Gospels: the Lord is not at once recognized; it required some word or familiar gesture to make him known. This is an effective way of stressing the point that Jesus had not returned to life as before but had passed, beyond death, to new life with God. He is Jesus, and yet he is different—transformed. Though, eventually, Peter will be solemnly commissioned (vv. 7, 11), it is not he, but the Beloved Disciple who is sensitive in faith to the presence of the risen Jesus and recognized him (v. 7).

The miraculous catch of fish, with its symbolic reference to "fishers of people" (Luke 5:10), is summons to an apostolic mission. At that lakeside breakfast, Jesus "took the bread and gave it to them" (John 21:13). His gesture answers the question of how Jesus is present to his disciples: he is present among them as they share the eucharistic meal.

In verses 15–19, Peter, who had failed his Lord (18:15–27), is now reinstated and entrusted with a pastoral mission. Peter's story is one of calling, falling, and recalling. It is noteworthy that he is entrusted with "my lambs and my sheep." The Lord is, and remains "the chief shepherd" (1 Pet 5:4); there can be no other. Peter asks about the Beloved Disciple: "Lord, what about him?" (John 21:21). The actual situation is that both Peter and the Beloved Disciple are dead, and the Johannine community is coming to terms with a new and difficult situation. It had linked up with the Great Church but continues to extol its revered founder. It is he, the Beloved Disciple, who is the source of their distinctive story of the life and preaching, death and resurrection of Jesus. He is an anonymous saint—and they are the best kind! As the conclusion of the epilogue, verse 25 is a conscious echo of the original conclusion (20:30–31). The Fourth Gospel is, indeed, a story of Jesus; it is not the whole story.

Jesus was arrested but on his own terms. He took command and was in command to the end. He spoke forthrightly to the high priest. The trial before Pilate is high drama as Jesus and Pilate dialogued. It became increasingly clear that Pilate was the one on trial. At the end, after thrice proclaiming Jesus not guilty, he condemned an innocent man.

Carrying his own cross, Jesus went to Golgotha. In a closing gesture, he confirmed the Mother and the Beloved Disciple as models of faith. Jesus chose his moment of death—the moment when all is fulfilled. His last breath was the bestowal of the Spirit. As Passover Lamb, not a bone of him was broken. A flood of new life, through baptism and Eucharist, flowed from his crucified body. He was given a royal burial by two erstwhile hidden disciples.

The Beloved Disciple was the one who understood the meaning of the empty tomb. Mary Magdalene recognized the voice of the Good Shepherd. She was sent (*apostolos*) to proclaim the good news. Jesus came to his disciples to bestow on them the Spirit—his new presence. Thomas became the occasion of our comfort: the blessedness of those who believe without seeing. This Gospel, like each of them, was concerned throughout with Christology and discipleship.

An epilogue narrates the rehabilitation of Peter and confirms the status of the Beloved Disciple. Both are dead. The good news abides.

Notes

1. Raymond E. Brown, *The Gospel According to John, XIII–XXI* (Garden City, NY: Doubleday, 1971), 843–96.

2. Francis J. Moloney, *The Gospel of John*, Sacra Pagina 4 (Collegeville, MN: Liturgical Press, 1998), 504.

3. Michael Mullins, *The Gospel of John: A Commentary* (Dublin: Columba Press, 2003), 391.

4. Moloney, *The Gospel of John*, 527.

5. Moloney, *The Gospel of John*, 343.

GLOSSARY

It is my hope that this glossary will provide the reader the meaning of some recurring terms that appear in the Gospel texts.

Abiding (*menein*) – "to abide," is a mutual and shared relationship. Jesus and the believer abide one in the other. It is from this mutual abiding that fruitfulness is achieved in Christian living.

Allegory – Allegory, in which the details of a story have symbolic value, such as in the Parable of the Wicked Tenants (Luke 20:9–20), is extended metaphor and, as such, is a story that has both a literal and a metaphorical level. An allegorical story can well be a parable, as in the example cited. There are several allegorical parables in the Gospels.

Apocalyptic – *Apocalypse*, from the Greek *apocalypsis* ("revelation"), designates a type of Jewish literature that flourished from about 200 BCE to 100 CE. As a literary form, it is presented as a revelation, or series of revelations, of heavenly secrets made to a seer and conveyed in highly symbolic imagery.

It is a crisis literature. The biblical apocalypses are the Book of Daniel (more precisely, Dan 7—12) and the Book of Revelation of John. Apocalypticism is the worldview of an apocalyptic movement. In this view, it is taken for granted that a supernatural world stands above our earthly world. That heavenly world is the "real" world. There is a twofold dualism: vertical, the world above and our world, and horizontal, our age and the age to come. There is always a definitive eschatological judgment: the final clash between good and evil, issuing in the total victory of God and the end of evil. Apocalyptic ideas pervade the New Testament.

Apostle – The Christian mission was carried out by "apostles"—those "sent out" (*apostellein*) from the Christian communities. Acts 13:1–4, the designation and sending out by the Antioch community of Barnabas and Saul, is an eloquent instance of this. There has been an unfortunate confusion of "Twelve" and "apostle." The Twelve were "apostles" in the sense that they had been "sent out" by Jesus. However, *apostle* has a much wider range than the *Twelve.*

Christology – Christology is the theological understanding of Jesus. In Jesus of Nazareth, God is really and truly present. That is the great Christian truth. However, to seek to define the mysterious nature of Jesus is a precarious endeavor. For centuries, it has been assumed that the fifth-century Council of Chalcedon had spoken the definitive christological word when it answered, in the affirmative, the question of whether God's salvation had been given, once for all, in the man Jesus. Because the answer had to be yes, and because salvation is of God, it had to be asserted, in the theological language of the day, that God himself was present in the man Jesus. That had been said, long before, by Paul: "God was in Christ, reconciling the world to himself" (2 Cor 5:19 NLT).

Covenant – Originally a treaty graciously "granted" by an overlord. God gave a covenant to his people at Sinai ("I am your God; you are my people") sealed and ratified in the blood of a sacrificial victim. Jeremiah spoke of a "new covenant" (Jer 31:31–34). This new covenant with the new people of God was given through Jesus and sealed in his blood (see 1 Cor 11:25).

Disciple – Jesus gathered around himself a group of committed disciples, some of whom were also active in the early Church. Distinctive features of this initial discipleship were the following: Jesus took the initiative in calling; "following" meant literal, physical following of an itinerant preacher, and disciples were warned that they might face suffering and hostility. The evidence is clear that some women did follow Jesus during his ministry in Galilee and accompanied him on his last journey to Jerusalem (see John 11:1–46, Luke 10:38, and 8:1–3). *Disciple* is an inclusive term.

Eschatological – Pertaining to the *eschaton*, the end. Eschatology refers to the new age, the transformation of our world. However, with the coming of Jesus, this new age has already begun; we await the consummation. In the preaching of Jesus, the kingdom of God is eschatological: the definitive intervention of God, his kingly reign, is (in Jesus) a present reality. It seems that Jesus thought of himself as the eschatological prophet. The Fourth Gospel tells us the eschatological being—the Son of God—has come in the flesh. He brings the eternal into the present.

Glory (*doxa*) – In the Fourth Gospel, "glory" has overtones of manifestation, revelation. The glorification of Jesus is in his passion, death, and resurrection. This is the supreme manifestation of the love of Father and Son for sinful humankind.

Kerygma – The "heralding" or "preaching" of the good news: the missionary preaching of the good news to Jews and Gentiles.

Messiah – From a Hebrew word meaning "anointed." In Greek, it is rendered *Christos*, whence "Christ" and occurs nineteen times in the Gospel of John. In Jewish expectation, the Messiah would be God's instrument (not a divine figure) in ushering in his kingdom. The expectation is a development of the promise to David in 2 Samuel 7:11–16—the expectation of a royal Messiah. In the New Testament, Jesus is "son of David." It is unlikely that Jesus himself ever claimed to be the Messiah. It is also very likely that Jesus' opponents may have understood him and his followers to claim that he was the Messiah. After the resurrection, of course, Jesus was, by his followers, regularly called the Messiah—Jesus Christ (Messiah). But he was a paradoxical Messiah: one who suffered and died on a cross, not the triumphalist royal messiah of popular expectation. John clearly links eternal life to understanding that Jesus is the Messiah (cf. 20:31). The language is not exclusive, and so cannot be read as supplying a universal requirement for salvation for all people. However, throughout the Gospel, those who believe that he is the Messiah choose to follow him, and those who do not, reject him.

Paraclete (*parakletos*) – "Advocate." The term occurs only in the Johannine writings—John and 1 John 2:1. The Paraclete is the ongoing presence of the risen Jesus in the believer and in the Christian community. The Paraclete will lead into a fuller understanding of what Jesus had revealed and taught.

Parousia – The Greek word *parousia* means "presence" or "arrival." In the ancient Greek-speaking world, it was used of the ceremonial visit of a ruler or of the apparition of a god. In the New Testament, it is used of the "appearance" or coming of the glorified Christ at the close of salvation history (cf. John 5:25–29). It expresses, in dramatic fashion, faith in a final act of God marking the goal of human history, and the establishment, in its fullness, of the kingdom of God. After New Testament times, this came to be known, somewhat unhelpfully, as the Second Coming of Christ. The earliest Christians expected this consummation in their own time. The expectation may be, and is, often present without use of the term *parousia*.

Pharisees – The Pharisees formed a religious and political grouping of devout Jews that emphasized detailed study and observance of the Law of Moses. They also possessed a normative body of tradition—the traditions of the "fathers" or "elders." While they acknowledged that some of these legal rules and practices went beyond the Law, they maintained that such practices were, nevertheless, God's will for Israel. They actively engaged in trying to convince ordinary Jews to observe these practices in their daily life. Much of what is attributed to Pharisaic teaching refers to legal rulings or opinions regarding concrete behavior (*halakoth*) in matters of purity rules, Sabbath observance, tithing, marriage, and divorce. The Pharisees lacked political power but would have had some political influence. As a major religious force, they enjoyed the respect of the people. After 70 CE and the destruction of the Jerusalem Temple by the Romans, as practically the only religious group to have survived the Jewish War, their influence would have increased. All four Gospels attest to frequent contact of Jesus with Pharisees throughout his ministry. Not surprisingly, this relationship was one of tension because he and they addressed the same constituency. Jesus would have challenged them directly and in parable. Yet, the Gospels acknowledge that some Pharisees were willing to give Jesus a serious hearing (see, for example, Luke 7:36–50; John 3:1–2). It is noteworthy that Pharisees are practically absent in all Gospel passion narratives. The death of Jesus was brought about historically not by Pharisees, but by a religious and political alliance of Jerusalem priesthood and Roman political authority.

Pronouncement story – This is a brief story leading to a notable saying of Jesus; the story is designed to focus on the "punch line." For example, in Luke 20:25 (NLT), the saying "Then give back to Caesar what is Caesar's, and to God what is God's" is effectively emphasized.

Scribes – The word *scribe* in Hebrew, Greek, and other languages had a wide range of meaning. Scribes wrote, copied, and guarded records for tax and military purposes, annals for government archives, and religious texts. Palestinian scribes in

Jesus' time were, in fact, bureaucrats. In Jerusalem, they assisted the priests in judicial and religious proceedings in the Sanhedrin. They would have played a secretarial role and, as in a modern civil service, some might have had a measure of influence. On the whole, they were "retainers." The Gospels seem to suggest that the scribes, as a homogenous group, formed part of a united front against Jesus. This is not historically accurate.

Sadducees – The Sadducees were a small group of priestly and lay aristocrats based in Jerusalem. They were theologically conservative, adhering to the clear teaching of the Torah, or Pentateuch (see Acts 26:6–10). The Sadducees appear rarely in the Synoptics and are completely absent from the writings of John and Paul. Since this group existed because of their political and priestly ties, when Rome destroyed Jerusalem and the temple in 70 CE, the Sadducees were also destroyed. Read more on that at http://www.gotquestions.org/Sadducees-Pharisees.html#ixzz3ZNC4HQ2A.

Son of God – The New Testament church confessed Jesus as Son of God, and in doing so, attributed to Jesus a unique relationship to God. Was the title *Son of God* bestowed on Jesus during his lifetime? In Luke, it is used by the evangelist at the baptism of Jesus (3:21–22) and again at the transfiguration (9:28–35). The angel Gabriel also announces to Mary that "the child to be born will be holy; he will be called Son of God" (1:35). Nathaniel, at his first meeting, called him the Son of God (John 1:49; see also John 10:36).

Son of Man – "The Son of Man" occurs more than eighty times in the Gospels and, practically without exception, as a self-designation by Jesus. Jesus used the phrase in a neutral sense to refer to himself indirectly. He likely had in mind as well the "one like a son of man" of Daniel 7:13 (ESV). Jesus was the human one, serving God's purpose and looking to vindication at the completion of his mission. Early Christians embraced the phrase, now regarded as a title. Jesus uses the title twelve times in the Gospel of John (1:51; 3:13, 14; 5:27; 6:27, 53, 62; 8:28; 9:35; 12:23; 13:31; in 12:34, his language is quoted back to him).

Torah – Commonly translated "Law," but better rendered "instruction" or "guide of life," the Torah is basically the Pentateuch, the first five books of the Old Testament. For the Jews, the Torah was the full expression of God's purpose for his people. Indeed, Law and Lawgiver were practically identical. In this situation, the Torah took on an absolute value, and one could concern oneself exclusively with the law. Luke's strategy was to show that Jesus respected the Law while he transcended it. This would have special relevance for Gentile Christians. Furthermore, for John, the love of God is the fulfillment of the Law (Rom 13:8–10), and this love is manifest in the person and presence of Jesus, the perfect fulfillment of the Law of love (John 1:1; 13:34–35).

Select Bibliography

GENERAL

Brown, Raymond E. *The Death of the Messiah*. 2 vols. New York: Doubleday, 1994.

Dwyer, John C. *Son of Man and Son of God*. New York: Paulist Press, 1983.

Kuschel, Karl-Josef. *Born Before All Time? The Dispute over Christ's Origin*. London: SCM, 1993.

Lyons, Enda. *Jesus: Self-portrait by God*. Dublin: Columba Press, 1994.

Meier, John P. *A Marginal Jew*. New York: Doubleday, 1991.

Pagola, José Antonio. *Jesus: An Historical Approximation*. Miami: Convivium Press, 2012.

Sanders, E. P. *The Historical Figure of Jesus*. London: Penguin Books, 1995.

Schillebeeckx, Edward. *Christ: The Experience of Jesus as Lord*. New York: Crossroad, 1981.

GOSPEL OF JOHN

Ashton, John. *Understanding the Fourth Gospel.* Oxford: Clarendon Press, 1991.

Barrett, C. K. *The Gospel According to St. John.* 2nd ed. London: SPCK, 1978.

Brodie, Thomas L. *The Gospel According to John. A Literary and Theological Commentary.* Oxford: University Press, 1993.

Brown, Raymond E. *The Gospel According to John.* AB. 2 vols. New York: Doubleday, 1966, 1971.

———. *An Introduction to the Gospel of John.* Edited by F. J. Moloney. New York: Doubleday, 2003.

Culpepper, R. Alan. *Anatomy of the Fourth Gospel.* Philadelphia: Fortress, 1983.

Hanson, Anthony T. *The Prophetic Gospel.* Edinburgh: T. & T. Clark, 1991.

McPolin, James J. *John: New Testament Message* 6. Collegeville, MN: M. Glazier, 1986.

Moloney, Francis J. *The Gospel of John.* Sacra Pagina 4. Collegeville, MN: Liturgical Press, 1998.

Mullins, Michael. *The Gospel of John: A Commentary.* Dublin: Columba Press, 2003.

Schnackenburg, Rudolf. *The Gospel According to St. John.* 3 vols. New York: Crossroad, 1968–82.

Quast, Kevin. *Reading the Gospel of John: An Introduction.* New York: Paulist Press, 1991.

Schneiders, Sandra M. "The Gospel of John," *Interpretation* 49, no. 4 (1995): 52–54.

———. *Written That You May Believe: Encountering Jesus in the Fourth Gospel.* New York: Crossroad, 1999.